New Directions for
Adult and Continuing
Education

Susan Imel
Jovita M. Ross-Gordon
COEDITORS-IN-CHIEF

Arts and Societal Learning: Transforming Communities Socially, Politically, and Culturally

Sandra Hayes
Lyle Yorks
EDITORS

Number 116 • Winter 2007
Jossey-Bass
San Francisco

ARTS AND SOCIETAL LEARNING: TRANSFORMING COMMUNITIES SOCIALLY, POLITICALLY, AND CULTURALLY
Sandra Hayes, Lyle Yorks (eds.)
New Directions for Adult and Continuing Education, no. 116
Susan Imel, Jovita M. Ross-Gordon, Coeditors-in-Chief

Microfilm copies of issues and articles are available in 16mm and 35mm, as well as microfiche in 105mm, through University Microfilms Inc., 300 North Zeeb Road, Ann Arbor, Michigan 48106-1346.

NEW DIRECTIONS FOR ADULT AND CONTINUING EDUCATION (ISSN 1052-2891, electronic ISSN 1536-0717) is part of The Jossey-Bass Higher and Adult Education Series and is published quarterly by Wiley Subscription Services, Inc., A Wiley Company, at Jossey-Bass, 989 Market Street, San Francisco, California 94103-1741. Periodicals Postage Paid at San Francisco, California, and at additional mailing offices. POSTMASTER: Send address changes to New Directions for Adult and Continuing Education, Jossey-Bass, 989 Market Street, San Francisco, California 94103-1741.

New Directions for Adult and Continuing Education is indexed in CIJE: Current Index to Journals in Education (ERIC); Contents Pages in Education (T&F); ERIC Database (Education Resources Information Center; Higher Education Abstracts (Claremont Graduate University); and Sociological Abstracts (CSA/CIG).

SUBSCRIPTIONS cost $85.00 for individuals and $209.00 for institutions, agencies, and libraries.

EDITORIAL CORRESPONDENCE should be sent to the Coeditors-in-Chief, Susan Imel, ERIC/ACVE, 1900 Kenny Road, Columbus, Ohio 43210-1090, e-mail: imel.l@osu.edu; or Jovita M. Ross-Gordon, Southwest Texas State University, EAPS Dept., 601 University Drive, San Marcos, TX 78666.

Cover photograph by Jack Hollingsworth@Photodisc

Wiley Bicentennial Logo: Richard J. Pacifico

www.josseybass.com

CONTENTS

Editors' Notes

There is growing recognition in the literature on adult education of the importance of the affective dimension of adult learning, specifically the role of feeling and emotion. Along with this recognition, the role that art and other forms of expressive knowing can play in facilitating adult learning has gained increasing salience, especially in facilitating transformative learning. For close to a decade now, we have been interested in how art, as a form of presentational or expressive knowing, is germane to holistic learning and transforming perspectives between learners and across diverse communities. More recently, we have been further stimulated by the experience of cooperative inquiry involving a diverse group of social activists inquiring into the role of the arts in transforming communities. Learning was fundamental to this inquiry question. At the same time, we were influenced by another issue of *New Directions* that sought to demystify art and demonstrate its use in the classroom.

Our motivation in putting together this volume was to continue exploring the potential of the arts for adult and societal learning. Much adult education takes place in settings other than formal classrooms. In fact, a majority of the graduates of our program at Teachers College define themselves as practitioners whose primary work settings are large public organizations (both for profit and nonprofit), communities, religious institutions, and government agencies. We are also aware that many practitioners of "adult education," working to help adults and their wider communities learn their way through the challenges of contemporary society, do not define themselves as professional adult educators. There is much to be learned by connecting the formal theories and practices of adult education to the work these educators are doing.

Hence, in conceptualizing this volume we recruited a range of authors in terms of practice and background. Some of the chapters are more analytical, others more expressive. Each includes a story of the author's personal experience with the arts. We begin with Abby Scher's description of the insights gained by the participants in a cooperative inquiry group inquiring into how the arts can inform community activism. Abby Scher's chapter can be read on two levels. The first is how the power of artists and activists inquiring together with the intention of helping communities reflect and learn can lead to significant changes in practice. The second is reflecting on the insights from inquiry itself in terms of how the arts have an impact on the work of educators as change agents.

Sherre Wesley illustrates aspects of the role the arts can play in helping adults learn about multicultural diversity by recounting the experiences of participants in a study she did in 2005. She discusses the learning space the arts create, multiple ways of learning with the arts, and suggestions for how

adult educators can make greater use of the arts in their practice. Kwayera Archer-Cunningham describes how Ifetayo Cultural Arts in Brooklyn practices a three-tiered model of community development that places art at its strategic center. Sherre's chapter demonstrates the use of art for learning among people coming from diverse communities; Kwayera's work is helping to build community across generations among the members of the African Diaspora.

Valerie Kinloch offers an example of how young adults looking at their changing community find art in the urban landscape. Their insights generate dialogue across generations regarding how residents understand their communities. Like Kwayera, Valerie's piece looks at the role the arts play in bridging generational diversity within communities and—quite interestingly—the role of youth and young adults in stimulating adult learning. Arnold Aprill and Richard Townsell's chapter also demonstrates the role of visual art in helping people look at their community. Their piece demonstrates how visual art can be used to empower people and change the power dynamic around community development.

Jean Trounstine uses performing art to create learning spaces within a context specifically designed to be confining and disempowering: prisons. She uses established pieces to create this space and context. Marie-Claire Picher, through her use of Theater of the Oppressed, has adults create their performance through critical reflection on how the social and cultural structures of the larger society affect their lives. In both Jean's and Marie-Claire's works, issues of power and who has it are central to the learning.

This summary highlights only a particular feature of each contribution, but what is evident is how similar themes emerge across settings. We pull together some of these themes in Chapter Eight. One dominant theme that runs throughout the pieces in this issue is how the arts can bridge boundaries separating people and keep those boundaries porous. This bridging has power for broadening the experience of the learner and for valuing the identity of the other while sustaining one's own identity. This, we have come to believe, is one of the most important challenges of the work of adult education in the twenty-first century, helping all of us learn how to coexist in complex, multicultural societies that are simultaneously diverse and cohesive. This coexistence requires the holistic learners that the arts can help develop.

Sandra Hayes
Lyle Yorks
Editors

SANDRA HAYES is a lecturer in the Department of Organization and Leadership and a doctoral candidate in the Adult Learning and Leadership Program, Teachers College, Columbia University.

LYLE YORKS is an associate professor and director of the Adult Education Guided Intensive Study (AEGIS) doctoral program in the Department of Organization and Leadership, Teachers College, Columbia University.

New Directions for Adult and Continuing Education • DOI: 10.1002/ace

1

This chapter describes the insights and learning produced by a group of community activists and educators who participated in cooperative inquiry into the question, How and when does art release, create, and sustain transforming power for social change?

Can the Arts Change the World? The Transformative Power of Community Arts

Abby Scher

Can the arts change the world? A group of organizers gathered in cooperative inquiry over the course of eighteen months in 2004 and 2005 to think about this question and answered yes, the arts can indeed contribute to changing the world.

The Inquiry Group

We were seasoned community arts activists who, for more than twenty years, had woven together new understandings of the world and its possibilities. We had experience working with people in an economically impoverished neighborhood of Philadelphia (Lily Yeh), in Chicago public schools (Arnie Aprill), and among neighbors of diverse backgrounds in Los Angeles (Nobuko Miyamoto). Joining them were "regular" organizers: the director of a Christian development corporation on Chicago's Southwest side (Richard Townsell), a woman active in a Seattle center for abused deaf women (Elise Holliday), the head of a San Diego union (Fahari Jeffers), an outspoken organizer of moms on welfare who defend their right to go to college (Diana Spatz), and I (at the time a media organizer in New York of immigrant, African American, and other ethnic newspapers).

NEW DIRECTIONS FOR ADULT AND CONTINUING EDUCATION, no. 116, Winter 2007 © 2007 Wiley Periodicals, Inc.
Published online in Wiley InterScience (www.interscience.wiley.com) • DOI: 10.1002/ace.272

The Dialogue in the Inquiry

Brought together by the Ford Foundation-funded Leadership for a Changing World Program, we had the chance to think about our work through "cooperative inquiries" organized by New York University's Center for Leadership in Action. Through site visits and six face-to-face meetings, we saw the power of artists collaborating with the wider community to create a new sense of possibility. Yes, our neighborhoods were impoverished by an economy more and more organized to suit big companies and the wealthiest among us. Yes, our government waged wars seemingly beyond our control. Yes, our communities were torn apart by distrust.

Still, we know we are not without imagination and resources. In small worlds across the country, community artists managed to weave new understandings and trust, making possible further action to take on what feels like overwhelming forces of hate. Community arts can be disarming, giving you a novel angle of vision and eliciting the power of your emotions and intellect at the same time. They can help make people reflective and open to change. They can create new understandings of ourselves that push ethnic boundaries.

Lily captured this process: "We take where it's broken and begin to work on it by planting seeds which are inspired ideas. Turn the deficit in a neighborhood and make it work for you."

Lily herself was an art professor who eventually left her job to work full-time in north Philadelphia. Together with community residents, she took abandoned, rubble-strewn lots and did not accept that they must be ugly. Starting with the children, she inspired the community with the idea that things could be different. The Village of Arts and Humanities emerged, acres of abandoned lots became sculpture gardens, and buildings became the home of murals four stories high. The village created a children's theater that tours the world, and it eventually stepped into community work that was not art-related, such as creating new housing and supporting business people in their own economic development efforts.

Nobuko, a dancer and singer leading the arts organization Great Leap in Los Angeles, brought together Mexican Americans, Japanese immigrants, Muslims, and others to tell their families' stories of migration to the United States, building common ground and enlarging the boundaries of what they felt to be their communities.

She also worked with me in Brooklyn for a woman's dialogue project, where we brought together Muslim and Jewish women, Latinas, and a woman from Trinidad-Tobago, all of us overwhelmed by our organizing—working on such issues as domestic violence in Arab American and Pakistani American communities, redevelopment without creating gentrification in Brooklyn, leading a school, and creating interfaith challenges to the government's repression of Muslim Americans after September 11, 2001. Her healing circles with storytelling and body movement made us aware of

New Directions for Adult and Continuing Education • DOI: 10.1002/ace

both how separated we were from one another and how much we neglect ourselves in our rush to nurture our families and neighbors.

"The arts open boundaries among cultures," Nobuko said, "but also among disciplines, generations, and faiths." Nobuko's cultural work rests on her insight that we all have to grow and change for the world that is coming. "The balance of majority and minority is going to shift," says Nobuko. "So we need to be able to create community between cultures—creating something new out of the ways that we are not the same." We need to "connect people and build interrelationships among our creative fires and imaginations outward through race, class, and gender to create real communication." At the heart of her project is a sense of urgency in creating respectful and new communities across our differences.

Arnie collaborated with Richard in his Chicago neighborhood of Lawndale to undercut the power of policy experts in a meeting launching a community planning process. Rather than running the meeting and setting the agenda, as they had expected, the policy experts ended up joining hundreds of community people in cutting out visual representations of their vision for the neighborhood. Then they saw their paper cutout pasted on the wall with those from the rest of the community to create a big picture of where folks wanted the neighborhood to go. It's not easy amplifying neighbors' voices over those of the experts, but Arnie and Richard managed it (see Chapter Five in this volume).

Those of us who are not artists were intrigued by the power of the community artists among us. By way of discussion, the artists saw their work anew through the eyes of the rest of us. Together we realized that all organizing is a creative act. All of us were stitching together communities fragmented by distrust, economic trials, ethnocentrism, and the silencing of our own knowledge by the overwhelming power of the media and what used to be called "the system." We fashion a new reality in what we create together.

As Richard said: "I had thought of the arts as a product—a mural, a mosaic, sculptures, or pictures. I now saw the arts as a way of thinking and making meaning in community."

Insights from the Inquiry

We came up with insights to share with other organizers. I wrote up our findings and offer a brief version for you here.[1]

Community Arts Create Safe Space. Community arts can create a safe space that allows us to trust and be open to change. We saw this in Los Angeles and Brooklyn, where Nobuko, a dancer and performer, brought together people from many backgrounds—Muslims, Buddhists, Arab and Jewish Americans, Chicanos, Dominicans, Japanese, and Japanese Americans. Through moving together and telling stories, they built trust and common ground. Through an arts exercise conducted with Arnie, Richard created another safe space in Lawndale. It allowed the "old heads" to step out of the way so the younger folks could take the lead, confident that the young ones had listened to the knowledge they would transmit.

Through the Arts, We Create Something New. The arts create a multiplicity of views that can offer many entry points for conversation and change. In the arts, we are each in our own way engaged in a battle against homogenization, struggling to build a new sense of ourselves, a sense of possibility, and a way of seeing outside of the ordinary. We start new conversations that cross beyond the boundaries of the commonplace and leave behind the platitudes created by the interests of the powerful. We are no longer consumers of culture, but its creators.

With Art, We Can Slow Down and Reflect. Art can serve as a speed bump, slowing us down to reflect. The process of creation—including writing and telling our stories—can help us slow down and reflect together, rather than talk past each other. Organizers sometimes jump ahead with their agenda before witnessing what is happening in a community. By slowing down, we unearth what is waiting to be spoken, and we clarify our core vision and purpose. This can help us hold to our true mission, whatever that might be.

Art Communicates and Envisions. Surrounding ourselves with beauty communicates that we are important and mean something in the world, while offering a vision of what we are working for. Lily brought her idea of "beauty is a right" to north Philly, just as Abused Deaf Women's Advocacy Services (ADWAS) instinctively did when beautifully decorating its Seattle office for abused, deaf women. Instead of communicating "This is a worthless neighborhood," Lily's art parks communicated "This is a place of meditation, beauty, and joy." Diana echoed Lily but was a bit pithier: "You think you don't deserve as much because you have a crummy school in a crummy neighborhood. You feel more worthy when you are surrounded by beauty."

Art Records the Past and Points to the Future. Art can honor our past by creating a record of what we have done, thus anchoring us for our move into the future. By reestablishing context, whether by naming our history, telling our stories, or making the community visible, we ground ourselves against the emptiness offered to us by mainstream culture. This is part of slowing down. It then allows us to distance ourselves from what is going on, so that we can make new things visible and recontextualize and analyze them. (This reminded me of the power of independent media, or at least its aspirations.)

Art Heals and Sustains. The process of creating together can heal and sustain us for the long haul. We realized that in this difficult political moment we needed to sustain our work by creating a healing culture within our organizations and movements that is compassionate to ourselves and others. Activists need some healing right now, and some of this may be done through the arts. We saw it especially in Nobuko's work. In Brooklyn, she and Abby brought together women leaders—Ecuadorian, Dominican, Caribbean, Arab, Jewish, and Japanese—into a healing space. By having the women tell their stories (sometimes in movement, by acting them out) and listen to each other with respect, she helped the hard-working organizers refresh themselves and open themselves to the struggles of one another and their communities.

Arts Engage in Community Transformation. The arts can make us comfortable with the role shifting that is part of community transformation. A Buddhist priest became a performing artist in Nobuko's Los Angeles creation. Big Man, a drug dealer and one of the leaders of the Village of Arts and Humanities, slowly left his old life behind and became a sculptor in Lily's north Philadelphia neighborhood. We need in some ways to become new people in any new world we hope to create, and the arts can help us work that out.

Art Brings Spiritual Practice to Harsh Reality. Through the arts, we can deal with harsh realities and transform them through the act of creation as a spiritual practice. Here, Lily and Nobuko both emphasized the importance of quality. Beautiful creation—not defined by museums or concert halls but rooted in "the heartbeat of the community"—lifts our spirits. Sophisticated expertise in dialog with the community can create this art.

Art Can Be a Disarming Process for Change. We also noticed that the arts can be disarming. Lily and her allies did a lot of their artwork and community development activities under the radar. This was not development driven by the vision of city planners. They created not a frontal attack but a subtler lateral move that did its job before the people in power noticed. A group that comes together around a mural can do other things: clean up a corner, register voters, exert pressure on elected officials, and redirect resources.

Don't Target Our Children—The Power of the Artistic Expression

Sometimes a frontal attack has a huge impact. We saw that in the Don't Target Our Children campaign, devised by Diana Spatz and her team at Low-Income Families' Empowerment Through Education (LIFETIME). LIFETIME members are moms who are struggling to raise their family, go to college, and defend public assistance programs, all at the same time. Diana sees her role as empowering women who are flattened by economic and family burdens to stand up and say, "We deserve better." It is a challenge, she says, not least because "in the midst of taking care of kids, you lose sight of the big picture."

One of the most empowering exercises for the moms came out of a simple task: "Draw a picture of what your education means to you." Diana showed that even those of us not working in the arts can draw on it in our organizing. "It made people really think," she said. By drawing a picture, the moms couldn't use the same old words that often come to mind. "Having rituals and a focus on the arts in all our gatherings expands our thinking," Diana says. Seeing ourselves and our realities in new ways is a key to change.

The Don't Target Our Children campaign brought the artistic creations of the members to the public in a successful effort to stop welfare cuts. To prepare for a visit to the California state capitol in January 2004, the moms painted political messages on 150 T-shirts, to neutralize the negative images the well-off legislators and reporters have of poor families with new images of strength and moxie. A child from Camptonville, in northern Sierra County, admonished Gov. Arnold Schwarzenegger with a small shirt that read, "Kindergarten Cop, I thought you cared about us!" On another, a mom had painted the backside of a baby with a bulls-eye in the middle of its diaper and the message, "Don't target our kids!" After taking over the governor's office, the moms won statewide media attention for messages such as this one from six-year-old Michaela Howerton of Oakland: "My back is too small to balance the state budget!"

Their creativity won the cause coverage in broadcast media and at least seven newspapers across the state, including the front page of the *Los Angeles Times,* which featured a photograph of the action with the caption, "Laundry List of Complaints." The event was also covered by the *Sacramento Bee,* the *San Jose Mercury News,* the *Contra Costa Times,* the *Inland Valley Daily Bulletin,* the *Los Angeles Daily News,* the *Honolulu Advertiser,* and *Sing Tao.*

Ultimately, the Don't Target Our Children campaign not only successfully blocked welfare cuts to children and families (and won the first cost of living increase since 1989) but also forced the media to see these mothers and their children as real people with value, helping change the political dynamic in the state. Through their art, the women and children transformed some ingrained cultural images that have a real impact on politics. They made visible the real context of welfare cuts: the pain they would cause to their families. Their art and agitation brought the accepted policies into question, opening up a space that allows other modes of expression, including moral questions, into a policy discourse that almost seems designed to shut them out. This opens up new avenues for popular power to express itself, even for those not versed in policyspeak.

Challenges and Limitations

Art builds on small successes. This is the organizers' mantra: come up with a small, doable solution—such as getting the city to install a speed bump that slows down fast drivers in a neighborhood—and then bigger victories seem possible. The same is true with art. You can't really fail at making art.

New Directions for Adult and Continuing Education • DOI: 10.1002/ace

By succeeding at creating something when job programs or economic development projects have failed in the past, you can build confidence, trust, and hope to take further risks and try other ways of changing your environment. You develop a sense of your own creative power and what it is possible to accomplish together. You are no longer a spectator on the world, but bringing your own expression and experience to it.

Yet we were all aware that our successes could also remain limited in scope. Our work could create big vision but small results, given the organizational obstacles we face today. We also recognized that people too often feel that their voices remain small and frail. We asked, "How do you nurture this voice outside the system? How do you maintain it coherently? Can a community express a sense of discrete identity, not just in relation to the mainstream?" It is a challenge to sustain the insights that emerged in creative arts organizing if we don't build institutions and locations where people can continue to act on them.

We brainstormed a list of obstacles that prevent the creative arts from being transformative. Here is what we found:

- *The class divide.* Richard reminded us of one of Saul Alinsky's insights (1989): you have to align the poor with the middle class, or the middle class will move to the right. Through the arts, it is harder to bridge the class divide than the cultural or ethnic ones Nobuko, Lily, and I have dealt with.
- *Funders' pace and cronyism.* "Our work is *our* work; it is not the funder's work." Program officers can be overly directive, or quickly move on to support other projects, creating a roller coaster for innovators. Or they find it easier to just keep giving money out to big institutions, which often don't have the capacity to work at the grassroots where the community arts are most fertile.
- *Older leaders don't give up control.* Outdated ideas can smother innovation, especially when they're held by leaders of a previous generation who control funding and other levers of power. This is a problem in every area of organizing, but also in the community arts.
- *The arts are seen as politically irrelevant.* More research and documentation of the impact of community arts in organizing can help reverse this idea.
- *Artists' egos.* Artists may begin to think that only they can be creative in a community. This is another version of the Expert Running Wild, and it is particularly treacherous while attempting cross-cultural work. Ideas of how to involve people are culturally specific. Artists cannot assume people buy in to their approach.
- *The arts are seen as risky or politically threatening.* The artist stereotype can work in artists' favor: they are into play and experimentation. But when working in partnership with a more traditional organizer, the organizer may pull back as play gets uncomfortable or challenges

New Directions for Adult and Continuing Education • DOI: 10.1002/ace

preconceived ideas or institutional power. It is, after all, a risk to open up your organization to the unknown—not just to unknown ideas but to unknown people.

- *The arts can be another form of mystification.* You can create an illusion of positive change in a violent and impoverished neighborhood by painting a nice mural. Or it can impose other people's values on a neighborhood, privileging some people and denying the reality of people's lives.
- *The transformative power of the arts too often stays at an individual level.* So individual people may become more open, expressive, and so on, but does that always help create a collective difference in the world? Well, no. But nothing is perfect.

Arnie also had some insights that were particular to the tension between established arts organizations (such as museums) and community organizing. Museums do outreach to try to bring new audiences in. Yet, he said, "The outreach model is a scarcity model, in which art assumes its value in direct proportion to its exclusiveness, placing arts organizations in the awkward position of struggling to connect to those it has excluded. This one-directional process tends to exacerbate ethnocentric assumptions about the cultures and capacities of the communities being 'out-reached.'"[2]

Conclusion

Our cooperative inquiry inspired us to see new ways out of the dead space that organizing for justice often falls into. Although our insights felt fresh to us, we also know we are part of a long tradition. The community arts movement seems to reemerge any time there is a movement for social change: in the settlement houses of the 1890s and 1910s, among workers in the 1930s, during the 1960s and 1970s (this last an era that Lily, Arnie, and Nobuko all emerged from and contributed to).

The example of the Highlander Center in Tennessee reminds us that new consciousness not linked to activity is just verbiage, and also that activity can help create new consciousness. That sounds a little like Marx: "One makes the world aware of its consciousness, one awakens the world out of its own dream, that one explains to the world its own acts" (Marx, 1967, p. 214). The creativity of arts rooted in community is one route to the new consciousness that is so vital to social change movements.

Changes in identity, enlarging your sense of common humanity with those who are different, and feeling more powerful both as an individual and as part of a group are all deep transformations. By weaving together new understandings in a creative process that has no monetary value, we can support a sensibility that goes beyond the market values dominating our culture. We can create an alternative to the harshness of contemporary political discourse that is so alienating to people. Too often, people working for social justice marshal facts but offer no spirit. We might shy away from facing ambiguity or from aspiring to the unifying moral vision of a Martin Luther King, Jr. By opening up a space through art—familiar to us from childhood but giving us a new angle of vision as adults—we may also be embracing a different ethic of listening and understanding someone with whom we disagree.

Myles Horton of the Highlander Center was only one person who taught us of the resonance of the arts and social change in the tradition of popular education. He and his wife always drew on local music in their organizing work in the middle of Appalachia. This validated the culture of the residents and showed there is wisdom in everyday knowledge. It helps build relationships of trust and solidarity so that people can learn to question, remake their thinking, and then fight to change the relationships that are dehumanizing them. In *The Long Haul*, Horton's masterful autobiography (1990), we learned to take the tools we have and the culture we know and find a common expression to unify people's consciousness for action and change. On another continent but in a similar way, Paulo Freire (1985) touched on these same themes during the period of decolonization in Latin America.

We live in a media culture. We are in a battle of ideas—and values—and the arts help create and bring life to ideas, making values visible. As Arnie Aprill said, "Organizing, at its best, is also a creative act, a spiritual art."

If we, as organizers, are to join the battle, we need to pay more attention to the creative aspect of organizing, and to allow community arts activism to transform all of our social justice organizing.

Notes

1. The complete report was published by NYU's Research Center for Leadership in Action as Arnold Aprill and others, "Can the Arts Change the World? The Transformative Power of the Arts in Fostering and Sustaining Social Change" (2006). The cooperative inquiry process was led by Lyle Yorks and Sandra Hayes.
2. Our report includes more reflections on museums, based on our visit to the Wing Luke Museum in Seattle. Its exhibits are created by community members; for instance, Japanese Americans interned during World War II recreated the inside of one of the huts they lived in.

References

Alinsky, S. *Rules for Radicals*. New York: Vintage Press, 1989.
Freire, P. *The Politics of Education*. New York: Bergin & Garvey, 1985.
Horton, M. *The Long Haul: An Autobiography*. New York: Anchor Books, 1990.
Marx, K. In L. D. Easton and K. H. Guddat (eds.), *Writings of the Young Marx on Philosophy and Society*. Garden City, N.Y.: Doubleday, 1967.

ABBY SCHER *is a sociologist and journalist who often writes about organizing, economic justice, and civil liberties.*

2

Through the arts, people holistically learn, interact with greater multicultural diversity than elsewhere, and form connections with others. Participating in the arts gives adults experiences, contexts, and tools to help them reexperience, revision, and reconceptualize multicultural diversity in their lives and communities.

Multicultural Diversity: Learning Through the Arts

Sherre Wesley

We live in a world of difference, and all indications are that difference will increase. In this complex, interrelated, and changing world, we are challenged to explore ways of coming to know difference; retreating into homogeneity and isolationism is not an option. Arts participation gives adults experiences, contexts, and tools through which to learn about difference. Arts participation broadens people's worldview, forms bridges that cross racial and ethnic lines, creates a special and almost sacred learning space, and taps into multiple ways of learning and knowing. I contend that arts participation is an underused way of coming to know and value the diversity in our complex, interrelated, and changing world.

In many ways, this is a personal story. I am a middle-aged black woman originally from New Jersey and have been involved in some aspect of the arts for most of my life. I *know* the arts have given me experiences and tools to engage with and learn from diversity in many of its dimensions. Among other experiences, I've danced ceili with members of a local Irish American community until my calves were sore, my smile was huge, and my awareness expanded. I've gathered energy from members of a Polish American community who appeared almost immobile until the music played. With the music, they found new life and shared it with me. I've had mehendi (henna dye) reminders of time spent with Indian artists, a pounding heart after an exuberant evening with African dance, and a lingering reverberation in my body from Puerto Rican plena. In a movement workshop with Chinese speakers, I've learned primarily through touch. I've discussed both

classics and new artistic works from European traditions. In addition, I've shared my arts and more of myself with people from many backgrounds.

Through the arts, I've worked with people of every conceivable belief system, ability, and socioeconomic background. I've laughed, cried, empathized, and connected with people with whom I initially knew of nothing else in common. I've forged cross-cultural bonds that created lifelong friendships. Art has become a common denominator. I have been given the opportunity to change, I have been changed through the arts, and I have seen changes in other people. As I gain a greater appreciation of how powerful the arts can be in our quest to thrive, grow, and love this increasingly diverse world, my desire grows to share these experiences. A few of the many aspects of this phenomenon are explored in this chapter.

To illustrate aspects of the role of the arts in adult learning about multicultural diversity, I recount the experiences of adults who took part in a study I did (Wesley, 2005) of participants in small and midsized arts programs of all disciplines in a community in the Northeastern United States. The adults in the study were, in equal numbers, people of color and whites, and people who participated through creating and through attending or organizing the arts. This article focuses on race and ethnicity as primary dimensions of diversity.

In exploring how arts participation can assist adults in learning about multicultural diversity, this chapter discusses: (1) The learning space the arts create, (2) multiple ways of learning with the arts, and (3) ideas and suggestions as to how adult educators can apply lessons learned and make greater use of the arts in their practice.

The Learning Space

Within the environment of arts participation, there appears to be suspension of some of the rules by which people engage with multicultural diversity. Art helps to move us beyond the familiar, both in how we see multicultural diversity and in the rules that apply. It also creates a cocoon of safety in which to do so. Arts participation appears to create a safe haven, a trusted environment that is simultaneously familiar and yet removed, where adults can learn about multicultural diversity. It is a context where difference is valued, greater diversity exists, and connections are formed.

Difference Is Valued. The arts espouse to value what is original and different; acclaim is given to what is unlike others. Nolan contends that one of the functions of art is to "destabilize fixed ideas and existing identities" and "help us move into a different space where different rules apply" (Jones, 1999, p. 3). Maxine Greene (1995, 2001) reminds us that art challenges and encourages people to look and see differently, and that imagination is what helps us see things as if they could be otherwise.

Not only does art encourage seeing another person's perspective, it encourages seeing societal structures and interactions in ways neither

New Directions for Adult and Continuing Education • DOI: 10.1002/ace

encountered nor imagined before. Art, and its celebration of what is different, opens us to the possibility of imagining difference as something to be embraced rather than pushed away. Learning to see and create and be with art helps us imagine without fear.

Greater Diversity. "I think the arts, in terms of racial and cultural pieces, tended to be more so—racially diverse and culturally diverse because it was the one place where people could reach out and extend themselves beyond their own culture, beyond their own racial background, and could enjoy music and art and poetry from a variety of sources" (Michael, male, person of color, attender [note that all participants' names are pseudonyms]).

This quote expresses the experience of many participants. Several study participants, particularly white people, noted that they actively seek arts events where they and their children can interact with people from other multicultural backgrounds. The majority (seventeen of twenty, or 85 percent) of the people interviewed for this qualitative study stated that there was more multicultural diversity in their arts arena than in their work, social, and community arenas. This is consistent with other researchers who have found that the arts involve interacting with diverse people and cultures (Jacobson, 1996; Singh, 1997; UNESCO—Institute for Education, 1997), and that the arts have a tendency to attract people from various backgrounds. More than a decade ago, Price (1994) observed the special nature of the arts arena when he wrote, "The tendency of the arts to accept and benefit from the cross fertilization of cultures has been one of the reasons why so many historically marginalized people have considered arts organizations as havens" (pp. xvii–xviii).

Arts create and situate people in settings where there is greater diversity than elsewhere in their lives. These places become generative learning spaces where people can share experiences and learn with people from multicultural backgrounds.

Connections Formed. "People who are interested in the arts, they just *connect* deeper to a person than . . . even their culture, their religion, their race, their social standing" (Theresa, female, white, creator).

Arts participation makes it possible for adults to learn about themselves and each other, and to make connections with the world. According to study participant Roger, "It gives you the opportunity to relate to people on a level that is beyond anything that we can explain physically." Using Putnam's concepts of bridging and bonding (2000), arts both bridge multicultural differences and strengthen bonds within groups. In one example, members of a Chinese community participate in their traditional arts as a way of maintaining bonds with other people from their homeland. They also perform and educate Western audiences about traditional Chinese dance as a way to create bridges. According to Yulan, a study participant, art is particularly effective in bridging cultural groups because "you don't need language. Dancing, music, painting—people can see it and feel it, and understand it."

New Directions for Adult and Continuing Education • DOI: 10.1002/ace

Embedded in both the bridging and bonding concepts is that there is something that can be identified as a common ground, common concern, or common experience. Arts participation promotes a "common" that is seen when bridging cultural groups, and when creating communities. After years in corporate America, Linda, an organizer of the arts, is building a new career. For her, "Right now, my only sense of community comes from the arts." Others join a chorus or dance ensemble to create, or activate, a common in a new locale.

There are personal connections made with another human being, and there are broader societal connections made. Without losing a sense of their multicultural background, participants appear to find in the arts a temporary opportunity to simultaneously feel their belonging to a cultural community and to an artistic community with people from other multicultural backgrounds. Time and again, people in the study, particularly people of color, expressed their connections with both cultural and arts communities. According to Bill, "Yeah, I'm black. And all those things that are black and all those things that have historically happened to blacks in this country, in this society, I'm well aware. And I can't use that eye to look at things that I'm doing. OK? I have to use a different eye to see where I want to go and what I want to participate in."

Bill's "other eye" is poetry. Merriam and Caffarella (1999) note that a "wisdom of the ages continues to be a fluid and elusive idea, which is most often characterized by the acceptance of ambiguity, as one of its many virtues" (p. 161). In the arts arena, participants are able to hold the ambiguity of being members of both cultural and artistic communities. It is a place where, as Goldbard (2006) states, "No story invalidates the others; all of them can coexist" (p. 1).

Laura, a black creator in the study, told a moving and tragic story of an experience where she was the only person of color in a huge theater, yet she added, "On some level, these are my people. I need to be with these people." For Rafael, a Latino painter, sharing a cultural background is not always as deep and engaging as sharing an artistic background. The value art gives to difference and its ability to form connections facilitate creation of a safe haven where people can hold their own ambiguity while they experience, reflect, and holistically learn. This ability to not always be either-or helps adults claim their own cultural heritage, while they holistically connect with people from other multicultural backgrounds.

Arts participation places adults in an environment with more multicultural diversity than other areas of their lives, but it would be a mistake to assume that there is no racism or prejudice within the arts. Issues of racism, prejudice, and stereotyping are very much a part of the arts experience. Among those closest to the arts—creators of all multicultural backgrounds—90 percent of those in the study have had negative key experiences involving the arts and multicultural diversity. Still, they remain engaged in the arts and return time and again to these environments. In the arts, people appear to find a place where it is safe to experience and engage with difference, rather than a place to shy away from what is unfamiliar, or even contradictory, to that found in other arenas in life.

One reason adults remain engaged is that they believe in the higher, unifying ideals of the arts. For many, art becomes something greater than the individual, something approached almost spiritually for its transformative qualities. For the participants in the study, art often unites to a higher ideal.

Multiple Ways of Learning with the Arts

"You have people from different backgrounds coming in to share this thing called art . . . who bring with them so many diverse situations and backgrounds and cultural experiences that you get to learn" (Bill, male, person of color, attender, and organizer).

Art embodies diverse ways of learning. It is grounded in the experiential, yet it is the integration of many diverse modalities that makes this learning most powerful.

Lawrence (2005) succinctly states that "learning through art is always an experiential activity" (p. 80), and current perspectives conceptualize learning from experience as involving a number of domains. Maltbia (2001) integrates several theorists to position learning from experience as "a holistic process characterized by work of the *head* (cognitive domain), *hand* (behavior domain), and *heart* (conative domain)" (p. 45). Fenwick (2001) adds the dimension of "unconscious dynamics" to her understanding of how adults learn from experience.

Learning from experience theory also informs us of the importance of context and what Dewey (1938) considers "interaction." The interplay and tension between the individual and the contextual is dynamic and essential in learning about cultures. As Jacobson (1996) notes, this is particularly important with cultural learning because "cultural knowledge is not learned *from* experience, but *in* experience" (p. 16). Arts participation creates experiences and a contextual safe haven well suited to holistically learning multicultural knowledge.

Learning through the arts occurs whether the experience is a hands-on one or involves participation via attendance. Both are experiential. Arts can be their own way of learning, or the stimuli for learning in other ways. This can involve planned discussion about multicultural content material, research of sociopolitical events to create a song or mural, or study of historical events to write a play. However, the arts experience is diminished if it occurs only in the cognitive domain. It is through the arts doing what they do—communicating and connecting—that one can have a deep learning experience. As McCarthy, Ondaatje, Zakaras, and Brooks (2004) note, "Unlike most communication, which takes place through discourse, art communicates through felt experience" (p. xv).

Art, at its best, does not stay on the stage, page, or canvas, or even at cognitive appreciation of the content. Art makes a leap, a connection that allows the audience member, as well as the creator, to have an experience transcending a number of domains. An experience as audience can be as life-changing (albeit different) as creating art. In the study, Kim, an organizer, told a story about an arts experience with a woman working with homeless children that "changed my life forever."

Yorks and Kasl (2002) state that when developing "empathic knowing amid diversity," one of the challenges is "to find ways of entering the whole-person knowing of others" (pp. 185–186). I have found that participating in the arts gives adults one route for entering a "whole-person knowing" of someone from another background. This happens, for example, when an actor portrays a character from origins other than her or his own, and it happens when someone feels totally and multidimensionally connected with the images in a painting.

Through their arts experiences, adults in the study were able to try on another person's point of view or culture, and they came to see parts of themselves in people from multicultural backgrounds. For example, a white singer was able to find a "little girl" part of her voice that she shared with a black singer, and a black woman found the parts of herself that she shared with an Asian male. The ability of the arts to allow "our imagination to be guided inside the other person" (Bennett, 1998, p. 211) demonstrates something Bennett suggests: that it "might serve to create a more sensitive and respectful climate for interracial and intercultural communication" (p. 212). I too have seen this phenomenon in my research and practice.

The arts can be the source material for critical reflection around multicultural diversity. Arts participation also can create a time and space for personal, "felt reflection," which happens when one's entire being is engaging with and integrating an experience. It is a time and space free from judgment, even from judging ourselves. One arts attender relished the opportunity to be still and quiet with herself following a performance: "I think discourse often leads—it can lead to understanding, but it can also lead to [disagreement]. I think the arts allow you to sit back, let it sink in, and *then* think about it, and then have the discourse" (Stephanie, female, white, attender).

As adult educators, we know that adults think and learn in many ways. Learning in and through the arts honors this multiplicity. At their best, the arts promote a feeling of empathy and connect affect and unconscious dynamics to the cognitive and behavioral. By requiring multiple modalities to experience and learn, and by not privileging the cognitive, learning through the arts can become a model of how to honor, value, and engage with multicultural diversity and diverse ways of knowing.

Art and the Spiritual: Uniting Through a Higher Ideal. "I think when you're connected by the higher idea of the art, whatever it is that you're doing—a play, a dance—you're just united with that person" (Theresa, female, white, creator).

As was mentioned, art can put people in prejudicial and racially insensitive environments, but it also constitutes a higher, unifying force that can encourage them to stay in and learn from the experiences in these environments. Most of the participants in the study acknowledged the spiritual when discussing experience within the safe haven of the arts, and how the spiritual aspects of art help them connect across difference. References are intertwined with other conversations, as when Althea talked about the "unseen hand" that directed her to stay with and work through material from an unfamiliar culture, or when Bill spoke of an arts experience as "uplifting." To Rafael: "You cannot explain how it [making art] works. It is something that is out of your reach. God is there. It's just the hand of God." To Althea: "The arts like that, music, dance—you cannot put them in a box. Because they are connected to a spiritual source, endless creativity."

Even where participants do not use religious language, the sense of a higher ideal can be found. For Mary, "Understanding and valuing multicultural diversity is a moral issue," and Deborah believes people get their moral and ethical "core" from the arts. According to her: "You don't even get it from church. [You] get it from sharing this view of humanity, and that comes from the arts." For example, art and the personal need to be honest when creating it are part of Laura's ethical core. It kept her worldly anger contained as she wrote a play. Laura, a black woman, commented:

> Even writing the white nurse, I'm always careful . . . I don't want to just put all my stuff on her. . . . I want it to be honest. I want to be true. And I want to hear what she has to say, because to me that's the only way that you're going to have real drama. . . . And I find that when I write these characters, that if I just tap into their humanity, that I will be able to create a well-rounded character, and not put so much of my *conscious* thinking onto what they're saying in their dialogue.

For participants in the study, art and aspects of the spiritual are often connected. Yet I initially felt uncomfortable using the word *creator.* It almost felt sacrilegious. According to Goldbard (2006), "[Community arts work] offers participants the opportunity to see themselves as creators, the role in which we are both most ourselves and most godlike: in the flow of creativity, we are enterprising, imaginative, playful, embodied, empathetic, excited, alive" (p. 1). When we are able to see what has not been seen before, know what has not been known before, and share what has not been shared before, we are being creators. Not all creators follow a traditional religious practice, but the vast majority (80 percent) of those in my study recognized spiritual relationships created through the arts. These relationships were with the higher ideal of art, and with the people with whom arts experiences were shared.

Application in Adult Education Practice

Following are a few ideas about how adult educators, including nonartists, can use the arts in helping adults learn a greater valuing of multicultural diversity.

Participation. We can participate in the arts ourselves. As adult educators, particularly educators concerned with social action and making the world a better place, it would be to our benefit to claim the arts as an additional way of learning and teaching. Vogel (2000) reminds us that "adult educators often choose to interact with folks who look and think like they do, therefore reducing ambiguity" (p. 22). Perhaps we need to take this opportunity, created through the arts, to extend beyond our comfort zone and put ourselves in a position where we are the "other" along a dimension of diversity. Arts participation can give us the opportunity to increase our ambiguity and promote the ensuing learning and transformation.

Educators can design, present, and give positive visibility to the arts of people who have historically been underrepresented. It behooves us to recognize and use the arts to promote programs that empower people who are sometimes marginalized. This enhances the personally enriching aspects of the arts for the participants, while furnishing a common point on which to bridge with others. Though arts participation is not a panacea, it can help people come to know what they share, and develop new perspectives about areas where they differ. It might help us educators, and the adults with whom we work, to be better equipped to hold ambiguity and embrace both what we have in common and where we differ.

New Relationships. Adult educators working in community settings can create opportunities to develop new understandings of community. According to Tisdell (2007), more empirical research is needed, but "it appears that engaging the cultural imagination can facilitate a greater sense of community, because it draws on people's authenticity and their creative power, which often relates to spirituality" (p. 11). Forums, both verbal and nonverbal, can be created as a place to learn and share across multicultural and artistic communities. Examples are programs where elders from multicultural backgrounds learned and sang each others' songs, and folk and traditional arts programs that highlighted similarities and differences between things such as hair plaiting, basket weaving, and net making.

We also can use a trip to a theater, gallery, concert, or other arts event to facilitate building relationships among members of business, civic, and volunteer groups. In one organization, members of a board of directors attend the theater together. As a result, they developed greater personal relationships and shared experiences through which they are able to connect in their organizational work. In addition, we can use the arts to interject more fun in our learning. One theater professional spoke of how much learning takes place when people are enjoying themselves, rather than being constantly "hit over the head" with a message.

New Directions for Adult and Continuing Education • DOI: 10.1002/ace

New and expanded partnerships should be developed between arts and social change organizations. Most communities have an arts council or discipline-based arts service organizations. Contacting such an organization would be a reasonable first step. As adult educators, we can forge these relationships to help learners and ourselves experience additional learning sites and partners.

Alternate Ways of Learning. We can use the arts as a model of learning through many methods, and not privileging the cognitive. As educators, we can design programs involving multiple ways of knowing and give adult learners a chance to just "be with" material for a time rather than immediately going into discussion or discourse. We can acknowledge the spiritual in learning and demonstrate what we espouse: to honor differing ways of learning.

Adults, especially those who have not participated in the arts in many years, might be hesitant to do so in a hands-on way, and this is where as adult educators we are charged with creating a safe and trusting environment for exploring alternatives. It can start simply: ask someone to diagram (not draw) differences they have experienced when a newcomer joins a class or club. Consider perspectives of the newcomer and those already in the group. Using Brookfield's critical incident reports (1995) as a model, ask learners to recall and communicate a critical image, sound, or movement associated with prejudice. Perhaps have a group illustrate power, or immigration, or disaster relief relationships through shapes. I have found that, particularly with the novice, the choice of words can be important. Adults are often less intimidated by words such as "diagram," "shape," or "move" than by "draw," "sculpt," or "dance." We can model the use of the arts in how we teach, not only in how learners learn. Also, I have found that not everything works in the way we expect. Our own ability to remain honest, flexible, and adaptable is called into play as we challenge ourselves to engage in new ways.

Expanded Understanding of Arts Participation. As adult educators concerned with social action, we should aim to make arts learning available as broadly as possible, particularly with adults who may historically have been limited in their access to the arts. Art is not only the province of artists, the socioeconomically privileged, or those who have been participating since their youth. Part of my goal is to empower "just plain folk" to participate in the powerful learning opportunities embodied in the arts.

Adult educators should take care to use a range of art disciplines, forms, and styles and not fall into the trap of working with and through only the "high arts," the very idea of which is contrary to the concept of honoring and valuing difference. We need to claim an inclusive understanding of art—one that appreciates the diversity represented by folk, popular, commercial, and emerging forms, as well as those based in Western classical traditions. All are possible realms and content for adult learning about multicultural diversity.

New Directions for Adult and Continuing Education • DOI: 10.1002/ace

Conclusion

Where it is used, arts participation can help adults come to value multicultural diversity. However, art remains an underused resource for adult educators. Within the arts arena, people holistically learn from experience, interact with greater multicultural diversity than elsewhere, and form connections. Empathy, the spiritual, and unconscious ways of knowing are all called into being and given a place of honor in learning.

Arts participation is a model of how to maintain social engagement in other arenas in the face of racism, stereotyping, and prejudice. Such things are very much a part of the arts experience, yet participants remain engaged and return to these environments. Among the reasons are the higher ideal, safe haven, and trusted boundaries created by the arts. Vogel's work (2000) with spirituality and adult educators found that "holding persons within boundaries helps them stay with the group issues under consideration" (p. 20). Where there is honesty and a higher goal, the participants stayed engaged despite racism, prejudice, and stereotyping.

Much of who we are is embedded in our arts. They help express who we are as individuals, and the multiple groups to which we belong. Because art can hold ambiguity, it is possible to honor multiple roles and simultaneously or sequentially belong to multiple groups. Through the arts, it is possible to try on another culture and come to see oneself as a person from other multicultural backgrounds. As a context for learning, there appears to be something special, protected, and almost sacred about the time and space spent with the arts. As one participant in the study said, art supplies a new "eye" through which to experience diversity in life. Art becomes a way to reexperience, revision, and reconceptualize multicultural diversity in one's life and community.

References

Bennett, M. J. "Overcoming the Golden Rule: Sympathy and Empathy." In M. J. Bennett (ed.), *Basic Concepts of Intercultural Communication.* Yarmouth, Maine: Intercultural Press, 1998.

Brookfield, S. *Becoming a Critically Reflective Teacher* (1st ed.). San Francisco: Jossey-Bass, 1995.

Dewey, J. *Experience and Education.* New York: Macmillan, 1938.

Fenwick, T. J. *Experiential Learning: A Theoretical Critique from Five Perspectives.* Columbus: Ohio State University, 2001.

Goldbard, A. *Higher Ground: Community Arts as Spiritual Practice* [electronic version]. National Guild of Community Schools of the Arts, 2006. Retrieved Jan. 10, 2007, from http://arlenegoldbard.com/2006/11/04/higher-ground-community-arts-as-spiritual-practice/.

Greene, M. *Releasing the Imagination: Essays on Education, the Arts, and Social Change.* San Francisco: Jossey-Bass, 1995.

Greene, M., and Lincoln Center Institute. *Variations on a Blue Guitar: The Lincoln Center Institute Lectures on Aesthetic Education.* New York: Teachers College Press, 2001.

Jacobson, W. "Learning, Culture, and Learning Culture." *Adult Education Quarterly,* 1996, 47(1), 15–28.

Jones, D. J. "Different Theatres, Different Audiences: The Arts and the Education of Adults." Paper presented at the SCUTREA, 29th Annual Conference, University of Warwick, 1999.

Jones, D. J., McConnell, B., and Normie, G. "One World, Many Cultures." Papers from the Fourth International Conference on Adult Education and the Arts, Cardenden, Scotland, 1996.

Lawrence, R. L. (ed.). *Artistic Ways of Knowing: Expanded Opportunities for Teaching and Learning.* New Directions for Adult and Continuing Education, no. 107. San Francisco: Jossey-Bass, 2005.

Maltbia, T. E. "The Journey of Becoming a Diversity Practitioner: The Connection Between Experience, Learning, and Competence." Unpublished doctoral dissertation, Department of Organization and Leadership, Teachers College, Columbia University, 2001.

McCarthy, K. F., Ondaatje, E. H., Zakaras, L., and Brooks, A. *Gifts of the Muse: Reframing the Debate About the Benefits of the Arts.* Santa Monica, Calif.: RAND Research in the Arts, 2004.

Merriam, S. B., and Caffarella, R. S. *Learning in Adulthood: A Comprehensive Guide* (2nd ed.). San Francisco: Jossey-Bass, 1999.

Price, C. A. *Many Voices, Many Opportunities: Cultural Pluralism and American Arts Policy.* New York: ACA Books, Allworth Press, 1994.

Putnam, R. D. *Bowling Alone: The Collapse and Revival of American Community.* New York: Simon & Schuster, 2000.

Singh, M. "Theme 1: Adult Learning and the Challenges of the 21st Century." Paper presented at the Fifth International Conference on Adult Education, Hamburg, Germany, July 14–18, 1997.

Tisdell, E. J. "In the New Millennium: The Role of Spirituality and the Cultural Imagination in Dealing with Diversity and Equity in the Higher Education Classroom." *Teachers College Record, 109*(3), 2007. Retrieved Jan. 10, 2007, from http://www. tcrecord.org ID Number: 12223.

UNESCO—Institute for Education. "Theme 7: Adult Learning, Media and Culture." Paper presented at the Fifth International Conference on Adult Education, Hamburg, Germany, July 14–18, 1997.

Vogel, L. J. "Spiritual Dimension of Informal Learning." In L. M. English and M. A. Gillen (eds.), *Addressing the Spiritual Dimensions of Adult Learning: What Educators Can Do.* New Directions for Adult and Continuing Education, no. 85. San Francisco: Jossey-Bass, 2000.

Wesley, S. L. "Role of Arts Participation in Adult Learning About Multicultural Diversity." Unpublished doctoral dissertation, Department of Organization and Leadership, Teachers College, Columbia University, 2005.

Yorks, L., and Kasl, E. S. *Collaborative Inquiry as a Strategy for Adult Learning.* San Francisco: Jossey-Bass, 2002.

SHERRE WESLEY *is an adult educator working with various educational institutions in the arts and diversity.*

3

This chapter discusses a three-tiered process of collective experiences of various artistic and cultural forms that fosters the healing and transformation of individuals, families, and communities of the African Diaspora.

Cultural Arts Education as Community Development: An Innovative Model of Healing and Transformation

Kwayera Archer-Cunningham

Ifetayo Cultural Arts, located in the Flatbush section of Brooklyn, espouses and practices a three-tiered model of community development that places art and culture at its strategic center. The first stratum of this model is the effect of arts and cultural knowledge experienced communally and development of a collective cultural identity. Having individuals and families united around a common set of cultural understandings, experiences, values, and modes of identification places the community in a position to continue growing and strengthening.

The second tier is educational. Ifetayo exposes individuals, families, and communities to cultures, histories, and attendant art forms that they would not encounter in conventional educational settings. This is the beginning of positive identification of self in relation to one's heritage. Supplying the tools for positive identification of self and heritage involves offering a curriculum that explores the cultural logics in which art forms are embedded and their particular social, political, ceremonial, and quotidian functionalities. The final tier involves promoting a sense of collectivity among individuals, which is accomplished through the collective experience of artistic and cultural education.

This chapter offers broader lessons for developing communities through the Ifetayo model of community development. Our process strives to produce one manifestation of the interconnection between autonomy and

NEW DIRECTIONS FOR ADULT AND CONTINUING EDUCATION, no. 116, Winter 2007 © 2007 Wiley Periodicals, Inc.
Published online in Wiley InterScience (www.interscience.wiley.com) • DOI: 10.1002/ace.274

25

homonomy made by Boucouvalas (1993). Autonomy reflects independence and uniqueness; homonomy is "the experience of being part of meaningful wholes and in harmony with super individual units such as family, social group, culture, and cosmic order" (p. 58, as referenced in Merriam and Caffarella, 1999, p. 310).

The Journey from Performing Artist to Educator

Ifetayo grew out of my own experience as a modern dancer with a prestigious and world renowned professional dance company. While under the tutelage of the founder of the Jubilation Dance Company, I learned many lessons that are the underpinnings of the work of the Ifetayo Cultural Arts center. Among these lessons was the connection between artistic excellence and the opportunity for healing individuals and the community, as well as developing the capacity for holding these two intentions. This was the early 1980s, I was in my early twenties, and I was not always aware of all that I was learning. However, this was the time of the emergence of AIDS and I was devastated by the deaths of half our dance community. The resulting disorientation led to my decision to stop my career as a professional dancer. It compelled me to bring professional arts into the community to raise self-awareness and esteem with African traditions as the vehicle.

The Meaning of Ifetayo

Ifetayo is a West African Yoruba word that means "love brings happiness," and it captures the core of what I hoped to create by empowering youth and families and building community. The organization's work is a reflection of values that have been historically upheld in African societies. Communities of the African Diaspora have always valued the contributions that every member of the community contributes toward its success. The high value placed on unity within the family and reverence for elders and for spiritual health is shared by individuals throughout the Diaspora. In addition, communities of African descent have always viewed the arts as integral to the spiritual, psychological, emotional, educational, and recreational dimensions of their lives. As a result, the arts and cultural learning serve as the foundation for the Ifetayo approach to developing communities.

Ifetayo takes this holistic approach to helping adults develop heightened self-worth, communicative skills, and stronger connections to each other, family, and community. To combat some of the obstacles to well-being experienced by the community members served, Ifetayo has developed a model for comprehensive community development that addresses the marginalization and disconnectedness that can come from one's inability to see oneself in the dominant community. Nothing in their environment references their heritage or reinforces the essence of who they are. The African perspective that permeates Ifetayo's arts programs begins to remedy this.

New Directions for Adult and Continuing Education • DOI: 10.1002/ace

For example, I recall one family that was going through a crisis. The child felt that only her friends had a family that was together and healthy. The father felt there was no model that recognized the hardships he was experiencing as a black man going to school and unemployed, decreasing his ability to provide the type of financial support the mom needed to care for the child when the child was not with her dad. All of the images the mother saw of black men reinforced her image of him as being a no-good man trying to get around the system of paying child support. He saw her as an angry woman with no understanding, trying to make sure he failed or seeking to get back at him for something of which he was unaware. This situation escalated his frustration, the mom's anger, and the child's isolation. Her parents had not been in the same room together since she was about two years old. Now thirteen, she was very depressed and her parents very frustrated. Further, the counseling they were receiving did not offer opportunities for them to celebrate their child together as adults. They had no supportive community to lean on when things got rough. The process of Ifetayo is to encourage gathering students in the program with parents in a supportive and nonjudgmental environment. The core values are essential for parents and students to agree on before going into family sessions.

Because of the child's membership in the Ifetayo performing arts ensemble, it appears that a true family crisis was averted. She had been contemplating suicide because of the hostility between her parents. Fortunately, as an active parent in the girl's life the father was asked to participate in a parent workshop that was designed to mirror the artistic experiences his daughter was having. Through her dance and creative writing experience, the girl was able to share openly about her pain. The father's participation in the parent workshop gave him a forum to share, for the first time, his frustration in an environment he found safe and supportive. His participation in the workshop opened him up to trying new things. Ultimately, this led to the father building enough confidence to interact directly with the mother after more than eleven years of estrangement. With the help of Ifetayo teachers and staff, the family had initially facilitated discussion on the center's premises. Later, also with the help of Ifetayo staff, these three people drafted action steps that led to ongoing interaction as a family outside the center. Through the child's participation in the arts programs at Ifetayo, the child and her family were able to rally. The parents have learned, and the result has been the saving of a child's life.

Theoretical Foundations of Ifetayo

The theoretical underpinnings and organizational praxis of Ifetayo reflect an African-centered (albeit syncretic) model of community development that places art and culture at the strategic center. It bears a strong kinship to and draws on the philosophy of Kawaida, enunciated by Maulana Karenga (1997), an ethos that gives rise to the core values of Kwanzaa.

Kawaida is "a cultural nationalist philosophy that argues that the key challenge in Black people's life is the challenge of culture, and that what Africans must do is to discover and bring forth the best of their culture, both ancient and current, and use it as a foundation to bring into being models of human excellence and possibilities to enrich and expand [their] lives." Ifetayo has become a leader in conducting research based on African Diaspora arts and culture programs and community development. These programs—and Ifetayo's strength—are rooted in long-standing and interconnected community ties with families and their children, as well as growing connections with an international community of elders throughout Africa and the Diaspora. As cited earlier, this focus of Ifetayo is consistent with Boucouvalas's argument (1993) that the essence of selfhood is the combination of the two trajectories of autonomy and homonomy. Rooted in the belief that selfhood has meaning in the context of community, Ifetayo anchors self-esteem and selfhood in a larger community.

Members of Ifetayo include those who are simply starved for opportunities to express themselves, or who desire to be part of a supportive community and achieve high personal, vocational, and educational goals. All of these realities make Ifetayo a microcosm for total reflection on the community and its needs. As a learning community, we engage in what I refer to as "responsive learning" and "responsive action." For example, we learned that we needed to go beyond using dance as the sole vehicle for connecting the community with its traditions. Over time, we expanded our work through the arts to include poetry, acting, creative writing, and jewelry making among others. Another example of responsive learning and responsive action at Ifetayo was our insight that, although youth is important to fulfilling tomorrow's healthy communities, the guidance and modeling must come from the elders in the community, starting with parents. The focus of many programs and organizations rooted in artistic development and exposure is often solely on the child. The key to creating true community transformation is using the significant education work that an organization achieves with youths as a doorway to parents and the broader community. That is why we have rites of passage programs and parent programs. We offer what the community asks for and do not just furnish what we think they need (Freire, 1990).

In a time when parents are working double and triple shifts to make ends meet, compounded by stressful realities of not living a balanced life, with few or no support systems, it is imperative that we investigate the realities adults are living under and how we can create opportunities for holistic communities, and healthy parents and adults. To achieve such a tall order, we must examine the manner in which children are currently learning. How they presently enter the world of learners is the formula established for how and where they learn and teach as adults. Community transformation is achieved by first establishing a safe place where adults believe they have something to contribute, ensuring that coming together

New Directions for Adult and Continuing Education • DOI: 10.1002/ace

with a body of people who have a common identity is paramount. This has proven to serve as an opening to nurturing change agents for self-expression, ongoing healing, and connecting with community.

In Ifetayo's model, adults are embraced as qualified members of the community with knowledge, traditions, and arts experiences to share with children, teachers, and the community at large. Having a multitiered process with a single effort is feasible and comprehensive. Encouraging adults to enter a classroom or an arts studio to share their cultural skill can create a shared identity and sense of value, as well as contribution and connection for the adults in sharing with teachers, students, and their own children.

The first phase of the approach is the effect of arts and cultural knowledge experienced communally and development of a collective cultural identity wherein individuals and families are united around common sets of cultural understandings, experiences, values, and modes of identification. This places the community in a position to continue growing and strengthening together. Gloria Ladson-Billings (1995) demonstrates similarly how parents are introduced to the arts numerous opportunities as expanded teachers and lifelong learners, contributing their skills and resulting in improved connection to their children while experiencing heightened self-worth and application of creative expression:

> Another way teachers can support cultural competence was demonstrated by Gertrude Winston . . . who taught for forty years. Winston worked hard to involve parents in her classroom. She created an "artist or craftsperson" in residence program so that students could learn from each others' parents and affirm cultural knowledge. Winston developed a rapport with parents and invited them to come into the classroom for one or two hours at a time for a period of two to four days. The parents, in consortium with Winston, demonstrated skills upon which Winston later built [Ladson-Billings, 1995, p. 161].

Although getting parents into class and sharing is part of the process, having them participate in their child's experience is the gateway to begin knocking down the barriers to finding the time, confidence, and desire to participate in artistic experiences that can continue developing the "new" adult learners. Including parents and family members in the educational and nurturing process through the arts has revealed an opportunity for adults who are in need of continued forums to share their knowledge and learn from those who may live in close proximity, actually creating connection familiar only to the former generation of elders. From the organization's inception, family members have come to specially organized classes, performances, and lectures designed to further reinforce culture and promote community support. In affirming the vital connections within family and community, Ifetayo chooses a policy of full disclosure both within groups and with the youths' parents. Both Ifetayo Youth Ensemble and Rites of Passage are about empowering youth, which the organization feels requires open communication on the part of both youths and adults (Stickler, personal communication, 2006). Among the adult population affiliated with youth, family and community development are conceived within a paradigm of collective sharing. The organization is committed to conferring tools for community and individual self-determination by offering programs in cultural awareness and performing and visual arts.

In the balance of this chapter, we focus on the adult constituent and how they become invested as self-healing community transformers.

Ifetayo's Approach in Practice

Eschewing the deficit model of "developing" communities, Ifetayo does not assume (and has never assumed) that resources for health and well-being lie solely in establishments outside the communities served but seeks them within these communities as well. It is this particular orientation to development that has been the formal basis of Ifetayo's strategic plans for community development. Ifetayo conducted extensive research, with the assistance of several scholars and community leaders, to identify the trans-historical locus of core values of African and Diaspora communities to serve as the ethical basis of all organizational programming and broader community development.

In many African Diaspora traditions, arts and culture are integrated into all aspects of society. Ifetayo takes this same holistic approach to encouraging community members to develop self-esteem, communicative skills, and stronger connection and responsibility toward each other, their families, and their communities. The commitment to conferring tools for self-determination by sponsoring programs in cultural awareness, performing and visual arts, health and wellness, and personal development is the foundation that Ifetayo has claimed as its roots.

The philosophy of the highlighted model has been further developed by adapting five core values as the philosophical foundation for our organization. The five principles are at the heart of the Ifetayo approach to serving urban community members through inclusive and responsive programs. These principles are integrated throughout the work of the organization:

1. Learning from the past is critical to building for the future.
2. The philosophy and mission of Ifetayo are integrated throughout the work of the organization.
3. Excellent teaching and program administration are the result of critical reflection and collective decision making.
4. Youths, families, and communities are strengthened and empowered when they are held to high expectations.
5. Communities are strengthened through approaches that are comprehensive and holistic.

By welcoming respected professionals who "come back to give back" to the community, we see that the beneficiaries of their artistic expertise are the families who are thus exposed to various artistic and cultural forms for the express purpose of engendering the healing and transformation of individuals, families, and community. The second tier of the model is education. With the arts being a key domain where a community achieves experiential and philosophical cohesion, harmony and growth are realized.

Mbongi: A Model of Mutually Constitutive Learning

Mbongi is a Kongolese word that means "learning place." It is a principle derived from the ancient empire of the Kongo but represents an archetype that is present in various societies throughout the world. As explicated by Bunseki Fu-Kiau (Bunseki, 2001), a Kongolese native and member of Ifetayo's Council of Elders and senior researchers, Mbongi is a succinct articulation of the idea that within every community there must be a dynamic, mutually constitutive, and ethically responsible relation between the individual and the group. *Mu kanda, babo longa ye longwa*: within the community everybody has the right to teach and to be taught.

Education Is a Matter of Reciprocity. True knowledge is acquired through sharing. Each member—with his or her unique attributes, opinions, habits, actions, and duties—contributes to the life of the group and must be committed to ensuring that each and all adhere to its core principles. Reciprocally, the group must support proper development of each individual and hold him or her accountable to the ethical standards that it espouses. As symbolized in the Kongo and in cultures throughout the world, Ifetayo invokes Mbongi in the geometric figure of the circle. The circle is a governing archetype of the organization and the actual form into which community members assemble for deciding organizational and programmatic policies and procedures, addressing grievances, and developing members of the community. The circle also reemerges in all of Ifetayo's programs; the participants begin and end every rehearsal or class in this formation. The goal of Mbongi, in both its general invocation and specific instances, is individual and collective resolution and healing.

In this model, the locus of the knowledge, learning, and resources that ultimately propel a community forward is distributed among and between the members. In Ifetayo's current application of this concept, although a teacher may be the recognized expert in a chosen artistic or intellectual medium, for instance, the insights of the student, parent, or volunteer may prove to be legitimate contributions to that teacher's development. In all of the programming, for example, participants are encouraged to be confident about communicating their sentiments to peers, teachers, mentors, elders, or other authority figures. At any moment, a member of the community, whether staff or participant, can call "Mbongi" to address an issue of concern. In calling the Mbongi, individual insights and grievances become not only communal knowledge but part of the collective experience and the ongoing processes of individual and communal transformation. One can see immediately how this culture of open exchange serves simultaneously to protect the participants in making the entire community aware of impending perils to empower these same participants to be agents and authors of their own individual and community interventions. The practice of Mbongi has allowed Ifetayo to uncover many issues concerning families and the communities, both internal and external to the organization, through which they navigate. When Mbongi is called, the entire community or the body of individuals involved in smaller subgroups (members associated with a particular program; administrative staff as an example) must attend to resolve the issue. In this forum, youths, supported by elder members of the community, are emboldened to respectfully address any adult member or peer. Although the issues addressed in Mbongis vary in gravity, the tone of these occasions is necessarily critical. It is essentially a constructive space, whereby ills are corrected, paradigms altered, and new modes of engagement are defined. Students may in a given instance become teachers of adults, and staff members may impart valuable wisdom to their direct managers. The liberating power of this tradition is further authenticated by Paulo Freire (1973), as he writes that authentic help means all those who are involved help each other mutually. This leads to people growing together in the common effort to understand the reality they seek to transform. It is only through such praxis—in which those who help and those who are being helped aid one another simultaneously—that the act of helping is free from the distortion in which the helper dominates the helped.

Every member, youth and adult, contributes to and benefits from this ongoing process of knowledge construction and conflict resolution through negotiation. This process has been responsible for routing out problems before they escalate, ensuring the stability, strength, and longevity of the organization and supporting the families it serves in a process of growth through candid yet loving exchange. What grounds the entire community and prevents it from succumbing to anarchy or a general crisis of authority are the core values and the understanding that every member must be respected and acknowledged for a unique contribution to community. In addition, praxis rooted in centuries-old tested and proven African tradition fosters a collective cultural identity. Ifetayo exposes individuals, families, and communities to cultures, histories, and attendant art forms that they would not encounter in conventional educational settings, instilling positive identification of self in relation to one's heritage.

Why the Arts? Creating Art-Specific Healing Spaces for Adults to Learn

The final tier of the Ifetayo process promotes a sense of collectivity between individuals, recognizing the intrinsic value of every member of a particular

New Directions for Adult and Continuing Education • DOI: 10.1002/ace

community to its overall health and vitality. This is accomplished through the collective experience of artistic and cultural education, with a central focus on individual members as agents of change and purveyors of knowledge.

Art has been a significant area in marginalized communities in America. Whether immigrant or native community, the arts have been used instinctively and historically for healing, celebration, ceremony, and socialization. The connectedness that is created when adults participate in song and dance or the visual arts is often overlooked and usually only seen as a great performance or party activity. The healing that comes from this activity reconnecting them with their cultural identity is rarely acknowledged by the larger society. There is an entire backstage process of living that is involved in creating ritual for community members to participate in art, which leads to informing and transformation and is carried over to families and the broader community. For initiatives working with youths with the goal of involving their parents and family members, awareness is needed in dealing with adults who are fearful, self-doubting, and less than comfortable about participating in an art form. This is where culturally specific arts activities can play a major role with adults. Embracing cultural traditions and using them as the point from which to embark can be an empowering experience in work with adults. Families who embrace their cultural traditions often see them as second nature, and not often as separate from the essence of their being. It can further be described as a basic fabric of how they communicate and express daily life. Having such a background filled with comprehensive effort to construct a paradigm for community transformation yields the experience of outcomes of healing, connection, relevance, and true community. Art in America is often seen as an exclusive activity; but even if one does not have money to go to the theater or partake in conservatory classes or the time to attend an open session at an artist league, there is often access to participation in something that is culturally part of community life, art at the grassroots community level filled with traditions, ritual, and reflection of daily success and challenges. The absence of this artistic expression and cultural alignment can compound stress and alienation and halt community building opportunities for individuals and families.

It is through efforts seeking to share art as a vehicle for creating transformation that this expression of daily life can become a tool for empowerment, self-identity, healing, and transformation. Art infuses the quotidian in the African mind—"If you can talk, you can sing; if you can walk, you can dance," states a popular African axiom—reflecting the universal Spirit in all things.

Music, dance, drama, and oratory are ubiquitous and central to the various ways in which a community interfaces with spiritual entities, marks significant transitions in life (initiation, birth, death, celebration), critiques and renegotiates sociopolitical realities, and opens certain avenues of physical, psychological, and spiritual healing. Conversely, the "art for art's sake" ethos is not a part of the African worldview. In fact, the arts tend to be woven throughout all aspects of life in various thriving cultures. Cardinal among the virtues of the arts is their ability to foster moments of productive communal exchange. Chiriqui Cooper, a graduate of Rites of Passage and a founding member of the Youth Ensemble (one of Ifetayo's core programs) who is now an adult, was hired in 2006 as program coordinator for the latter. Describing the intimate bond that creative immersion with a group of her peers afforded her, she states: ". . . These girls weren't just people I danced with, but were my sisters in pain and triumph. . . . No one was allowed half-stepping. Because this became a second family, we went through the trying times of trying to keep that family together" (Stickler, personal communication, 2006).

Granting individuals direct access to the most euphoric chambers of their personal and collective experiences, the arts help a community apprehend and experience itself as a loving, healthy, and productive aggregate of members striving for common elevation. Equally essential to the health of the community is a forum, a safe space within which the perceived obstacles to the work of community can be aired with the goal of resolution in mind. To this end, Ifetayo has embraced the African concept of Mbongi, the circle of learning.

As described by Bunseki Fu-Kiau (1985), Mbongi is not only a politico-educational institution; it is also a strong and lovely model of a common household. It is the "shaper" of the community leadership of the African traditional life. All issues of public interest, be they social, political, or economic, must be openly and publicly discussed. This is the teaching of the traditional political wisdom of Mbongi.

Culture and Art-Based Transformation. What distinguishes Ifetayo from many organizations that provide comprehensive community development services is a central focus on the holistic nurturing of members through the arts, the insistence on family and community inclusion and support, and the research-grounded embrace of time-honored African philosophical modalities on which the journey is based. With the guidance of world-renowned teachers, mentors, and scholars, all of whom have ongoing, intimate connection with the organization's programming, members are exposed to a panoply of artistic, cultural, and intellectual traditions. The organization's philosophy of learning positions youths and parents alongside familial and tutelary elders, as the authors and agents of their own personal, family, and community change.

Ifetayo conducted extensive research with the assistance of several scholars and community leaders to extract what we define as the core values of communities of the African Diaspora trans-historically to serve as the ethical basis of all of our organizational programming. As a result of this initial research (which will never officially reach its conclusion), Ifetayo made several discoveries that serve as defining features for our particular model of community development, three of which have been emphasized in this chapter: (1) the value of every member of a particular community for its overall health and vitality, (2) the central focus on youths as agents of change and purveyors of knowledge, and (3) the arts as the domain where a community achieves experiential and philosophical cohesion. In elaborating on these ideas, it is our goal to contribute to existing discussion about innovative methodologies and paradigms for doing development work.

Redefining the Place of the Arts in Community Development Paradigms

We are in a dance class. Pupils observe dancers in the lines that go before them, culling ideas on how the step might be best executed. As an individual dancer marries passion and technique with attendant honing of memory, discipline, and courage, it is common practice in African dance for the dance teacher to urge the line to "stay together. Feel each other as you cross the floor." The cohesion a participant encourages is as much a part of the dance class as is learning the steps. It betokens a cultural ideal but possesses more than mere semiotic significance. It implies an epistemological leap that translates a way of being within an instructional arena to a wider context: the coordination and sensitivity to each other that the dancers develop carries over beyond the confines of the class setting. Paradigms shift, connection is forged, the stage is set for creative work.

The process of youth and community development is never fixed at Ifetayo. It is a creative process of negotiation between the self and the social (milieu) that acknowledges identity as historically determined, looks to the past for foundation and inspiration, and then builds on it (Stickler, personal communication).

In a culture where anti-intellectualism, shallow thinking, and superficial exploration are rife, Ifetayo demands deep and rigorous interrogation of self, history, and ideas. In a place where the historical currents of racism and sexism induce low self-esteem that clouds vision and twists behavior, Ifetayo creates a safe space to explore fears and pain and to use the arts as a thrust toward growth grounded in honesty, fostering of collective experience, cathartic utterance of truth, and comprehensive and conscious balancing of community. As bell hooks (1994) describes: ". . . Learning is a place where paradise can be created . . . (where) we have the opportunity to labor for freedom, to demand of ourselves and our comrades, an openness of mind and of heart that allows us to face reality even as we collectively imagine ways to move beyond boundaries, to transgress. This is education as the practice of freedom" (p. 207).

Conclusion

Ifetayo's mission continues to embrace the families and larger community, always directing all efforts back to the whole and reinforcing the concept that individuals are whole only with each other. By preparing community members for all aspects of their lives through comprehensive and wide-ranging programs that help to empower them to become self-sufficient, yet connected to each other, Ifetayo encourages their active engagement in the improvement of their communities. This mission is carried out as Ifetayo works to achieve the five primary objectives of the organization:

1. Develop cultural awareness and self-esteem by exposing families to traditional African artistic forms and their evolution into contemporary cultures.
2. Give families and communities of African descent the tools to become self-sufficient and transcend challenges that are perpetuated across generations.
3. Support families and communities of African descent to reach their optimum potential by attaining harmonious balance among the mind, body, and spirit and through proper nutrition, exercise, and cultural awareness.
4. Create leaders for local neighborhoods and international communities.
5. Develop, document, and disseminate a comprehensive, African-centered approach to youth and community development.

References

Boucouvalas, M. "Consciousness and Learning: New and Renewed Approaches." In S. B. Merriam (ed.), *An Update on Adult Learning Theory*. New Directions for Adult and Continuing Education, no. 57. San Francisco: Jossey-Bass, 1993.

Bunseki Fu-Kiau, K. K. *The Mbongi, an African Traditional Political Institution*. Nyangew, Zaire: Omenana, 1985.

Bunseki Fu-Kiau, K. K. *Tying the Spiritual Knot: African Cosmology of the Bantu-Kongo Principles of Life and Living* (2nd ed.). Brooklyn, N.Y.: Athelia Henrietta Press, 2001.

Freire, P. *Education for Critical Consciousness*. New York: Seabury, 1973.

Freire, P. *Pedagogy of the Oppressed*. New York: Continuum, 1990.

hooks, b. *Teaching to Transgress: Education as the Practice of Freedom*. New York: Routledge, 1994.

Karenga, M. *Kwanzaa: A Celebration of Family, Community, and Culture*. Los Angeles: University of Sankore Press, 1997.

Ladson-Billings, G. "But That's Just Good Teaching! The Case for Culturally Relevant Pedagogy." *Theory into Practice*, 1995, *34*(3), 159–165.

Merriam, S. B., and Caffarella, R. S. *Learning in Adulthood: A Comprehensive Guide* (2nd ed.). San Francisco: Jossey-Bass, 1999.

KWAYERA ARCHER-CUNNINGHAM *is the founding executive director of Ifetayo Cultural Arts in Brooklyn, New York.*

New Directions for Adult and Continuing Education • DOI: 10.1002/ace

This article describes how two African American young adults engage in learning and activism in their Harlem community through employment of art forms. Observations on the reversal of learning—from adults to young people in classrooms and young people to adults in the community— are critiqued.

Youth Representations of Community, Art, and Struggle in Harlem

Valerie Kinloch

In the last twenty-five years, efforts to remedy urban decline and fortification of major U.S. cities have resulted in plans for revitalization through gentrification. Images of urban cities (Chicago, Cleveland, Detroit, New York, San Francisco) in disrepair have been sprawled across national magazines, billboards, and news reports. Pictures of abandoned buildings, homelessness, and racialized poverty are indicators of a large systemic problem representative of how public understanding of *urban* has reshifted from signifying "features of social organization—including a sense of community, positive neighborhood identification, and explicit norms and sanctions against aberrant behavior" (Wilson, 1987, p. 3) to qualities of "ferment, paradox, conflict, and dilemma" (Clark, 1965, p. 11). This shift indicates how popular narratives of urban are attentive to culprits of decline: crime, unemployment, abandoned space, lack of civic participation, and lost artistic renaissances.

According to Beauregard (1993), a focus on the culprits overlooks "the material contradictions and the cultural ambivalences that make large cities the sites for decay, disinvestment, and degeneracy" (p. 305). This way of seeing urban cities does not encourage multiple narratives of space; it does not take into consideration struggles, identities, and lived experiences of

This research project is funded by a grant from The Spencer Foundation and a Grant-in-Aid from the National Council of Teachers of English.

people who reside within, and may be displaced from, their community. Instead, it escapes "the material contradictions" of such communities, an act that reiterates decline over renewal, segregation over collaboration, and silent struggle over shared narratives of struggle. Even more dangerous is how the escape from contradiction embraces "normalization," which, according to Foucault (1984), imposes homogeneity by encouraging people "to determine levels, to fix specialties, and to render the differences useful by fitting them one to another" (p. 197). Foucault's attack on normalization and Beauregard's attention to contradictions are grounded in a perpetual search for truths across boundaries. Such truths (that is, urban landscapes and signs of decline; gentrified communities and calls for newness), I argue, may result from the transformative power of art. In what ways, then, can reimagination of urban from ferment, abandoned, and normalized to positive, artistic, and contradictory contribute to enhanced understanding of the value of such communities? What do local stories tell about the history and resurgence of art in communities facing current efforts of gentrification, renewal, and reproduction of space? Specifically, what impact do youths who use art to document community experiences have on adult learning?

The purpose of this chapter is to examine, through the lens of postmodernism and critical social theory, how young people employ art forms for transformative reasons, which in turn can influence adult learning and activism. By participating in their community in ways that galvanize historical struggles and cultural resources, youths enact a reversal of learning whereby they are educating adults in their community about tensions that exist in the interstices of discourse on urban revitalization and gentrification. In this chapter, I discuss tensions and learning reversals by illustrating how two African American teenagers, Quentin and Kavon, document art forms—through mapping, photography, and video interviews—in Harlem by being attentive to visible signs of decline and responsive to the community's reconceptualization of art. Then I explore how the young men confront the politics of space as they challenge normalization while influencing the learning of adults in the wider community. To do this, they have expanded their definition of art from "poetry, music, paintings, and museums" to "songs of human struggles, tools that stimulate community conversations, and visible signs of everyday life—housing projects, abandoned storefronts, 'rubble,' and the busy 125th Street thoroughfare connecting Harlem's west-side to its east-side." Dewey's artistic aesthetic or "art as experience" (1959) is a basic principle in this definition.

Context: Setting, Participants, and Data Collection

Quentin and Kavon were participants in a larger ethnographic project in an urban high school and community in Harlem. The students attending the

New Directions for Adult and Continuing Education • DOI: 10.1002/ace

school, which is known for its social justice mission, were from poor and working-class backgrounds and identified primarily as African, African American, and Latino. In the larger project, I investigate how youth perceptions of literacy connect to the politics of space, including classroom space and the surrounding Harlem community, and how such connections are rooted in sociopolitical struggles. By working with students in school and out-of-school spaces, I am able to identify shifting patterns in disposition toward success, embedded in a discourse of rights, power, and struggle across spatial contexts.

In the larger project, I was a participant-observer in three junior- and senior-level English classrooms for one and a half years. I observed students' responses to literacy activities such as readings, individual and group writings, performances, and teacher- or student-led discussion. The teacher and many of the students embraced my political perspective on the educational success of students of color—a perspective that emphasized student voice, choice, and awareness of the economic differences that oftentimes separate many urban students from their wealthier, and white, suburban peers. This perspective, grounded in postmodern and critical social theories, continuously evolved from regular interaction with students, many of whom felt that their voices were not appreciated and thus silenced by the adult members in their school and home communities. This latter point served as the basis for a smaller study on youth representations of community, art, and struggle in Harlem.

Quentin and Kavon became active participants in this current study. Concerned with disparities between "black students/black communities like Harlem that'll soon be gentrified and white students/white communities like the Upper East Side that's a different world," Quentin, Kavon, and I initiated a youth-based project on the art of Harlem that would be a response against gentrification. Together, we created shared rhyme books, which served as our paper space to pose and respond to questions on the art and struggles within Harlem. From our rhyme books, videotaped community documentaries, response to survey questions, and participation in community action planning meetings, we engaged in data-member checking sessions (Lincoln and Guba, 2000), shared analysis discussion, and interview meetings. During these sessions, we discussed the value of youngsters responding to community changes in ways that can influence adults (myself included) to "take action."

Quentin and Kavon, who live in close proximity to and have a fondness for Harlem's famous 125th Street, have been engaging in a process of transformation that involves reseeing their community from "in neglect" to a site where "art is in constant process" (Quentin). In a clip from his video documentary of the community, Kavon makes the comment, "Harlem is already art. It has been for decades, although the community is now being gentrified to create a sense of art [Quentin interrupts: "a fake sense of art"].

If this new art and new Harlem is going to improve our community, then why is it displacing so many of the black residents who've lived here for years?" Quentin cannot help but respond, "That's why we have to do this project on art in Harlem. It's time that young people stand up and talk about the value of Harlem. Look, where else can you find so many symbols of blackness in one community?"

The symbols that Quentin alludes to include the Apollo Theater, the Studio Museum of Harlem, and the Adam Clayton Powell Building on 125th Street. He is also referring to the Schomburg Center for Research in Black Culture, the Thurgood Marshall High School, the Harriet Tubman houses, the Frederick Douglass housing developments, and inscribed passages from speeches by Malcolm X that appear on the sides of buildings just as much as they appear on T-shirts worn by young and adult residents of Harlem. For Quentin and Kavon, these indicators of community art forms are significant. Also important are the values of stories, embedded in a struggle for rights, of Quentin, Kavon, and countless other urban youths about community and art. As argued throughout this chapter, honest, descriptive stories of young people can challenge negative images of urban (Beauregard, 1993) at the same time they inform adult learning and activism. Attention to youth voices reveals the importance of intergenerational collaboration, which has implications for improvement and protection of communities and for youth activism and adult leadership. This chapter, then, is responsive to how young people document their experiences in the geographical, postmodern landscape of Harlem by being attentive to struggles, sociopolitical tensions, and transformation of people and spaces.

Brief Review of Literature

Soja (1990) examines the social production of space by associating it with knowledge and power to posit a definition for postmodern geography. He argues that geography plays an important role in how history is documented and represented: "A distinctively postmodern and critical human geography is taking shape, brashly reasserting the interpretative significance of space in the historically privileged confines of contemporary critical thought" (p. 11). Social production of space involves interpretive qualities, material realities, and actual practices of and within space, or what Keith and Pile (1993) refer to as spatial metaphors: "global-local," "location," "third space," "the city" (p. 1). Spatial metaphors define space as always in a process in which meaning and experience are created, narrated, reproduced, and represented; hence, the existing tension between normalized and contradictory spaces. The proliferation of spatial metaphors and spatialization of contemporary social theory reiterate the value of space in the context of everyday life in terms of how pedagogy, identity, and human reality are situated in configurations of space and place.

New Directions for Adult and Continuing Education • DOI: 10.1002/ace

This latter point is reiterative of Freire's consideration (1970/1995) of the situationality of people who are oppressed by "temporal-spatial" conditions of human existence. Although Freire does not thoroughly investigate spatial aspects of situationality, he does indicate that it signifies philosophical recognition of the conditions of existence, geographical and contextual, that create learners, "cultural workers," who question themselves by engaging in action. Action, or what critical theorists name social transformation, establishes important relationships between critical pedagogy and theories of space and place. People exist in space, according to Freire, because of marked locatedness in situations of "reflection" and "discovery" (p. 90), an argument that connects to scholarship on postmodern geography (Soja, 1990; Keith and Pile, 1993; Castells, 1983) insofar as space, a "politics of location," is associated with cultural identity and historical representation. Such association encourages people to engage in reflection on, discovery of, and action in the very spaces they inhabit and travel through, including home space, school space, and work space. This engagement, informed by theories in social transformation (Giroux, 1992; McLaren, 1993), is reflective of how discourses of critical pedagogy and postmodern geography are concerned with ensuing conditions that shape and give meaning to people's involvement with space. Freire's interest (1998) in *reading the world* as a way to increase critical consciousness, particularly of oppressed people, sets the stage for additional scholarship on critical pedagogy that examines *conscientizacāo* (that is, cultural workers) who study contradictions of the world to engage in action.

Haymes (1995) explores the contradictory nature of space by articulating a "pedagogy of place" along theories of race, location, and social struggle in the lives of black urban residents. Drawing on racialized critical geography and critical social theory, Haymes is invested in promoting "critical narratology" (McLaren, 1993) and "critical multiculturalism" (Giroux, 1994) in educational research. His investment is motivated by an interest in urban residents' narrating stories of struggle and engaging in social transformation that teaches decolonization of limiting positions of power. Haymes establishes connections among pedagogy, the production of space, and power by interrogating definitions of "urban," "black," and "culture." He explicitly focuses on narratives of lived experiences by critiquing whiteness as connected to race (black) and place (urban communities) in promoting radical multiculturalism.

Haymes's work addresses dilemmas of transformation encountered by black urban residents, whom he encourages to redefine the spatial meanings of their living spaces: "Because inner-city blacks live on the margins of white supremacist domination and privilege, they have no other alternative than to struggle for the transformation of their places on the margin into spaces of cultural resistance" (p. 113). The push for cultural resistance speaks to critical pedagogy's emphasis on the fabric that creates situationality:

sociopolitical rendering of postmodern geographies, the transformative nature of temporal-spatial conditions, and the value that narrating positive stories of place has on the identity of young people and adults in urban communities. Haymes's research (1995) as well as that of Soja (1990) and Freire (1970/1995) reveal an urgency for scholarship that investigates the situationality of people in public spaces who envision community to be a major site of social, political, and economic mobility. This way of seeing contradicts traditional notions of urban as meaning in decline and in need of gentrification.

Connecting the Literature to the Current Study

Quentin and Kavon are aware of how cultural practices are inscribed, however unfairly, in dominant narratives of spatial signifiers (urban as poor; suburban as wealthy). They accept Soja's insistence (1990) that space is created to conceal consequences because "relations of power and discipline are inscribed into the apparently innocent spatiality of social life" (p. 6). In this acceptance, they grapple with ways to encourage adult members of the community to use art (such as billboard campaigns, local museums, historical buildings. avenues and boulevards, and other visible signs of change) to improve the area. They want adults to reclaim a positive community identity and willingly cross borders by understanding that the historical construction of borders, cultural and physical, both prohibits and permits "particular identities, individual capacities, and social forms" (Giroux, 1992, pp. 29–30).

Quentin and Kavon exert influence over their urban community by using photography and video interviews to capture temporal-spatial conditions in the postmodern landscape of Harlem. This chapter presents a brief glimpse into how they document the aesthetics of their community and their black situationality (Haymes, 1995) against the backdrop of adult efforts to reclaim artistic value in Harlem.

The Study with Quentin and Kavon

QUENTIN: See, the hard part of this project on Harlem and art is facing all the new people who are not even from Harlem and who think this community is all about the new things popping up: the Disney Store [now closed], the Magic Johnson Theater, Old Navy, Aerosoles [shoe store], and MAC [cosmetic store]. By the way, I wonder how many people now coming into Harlem know that right around the corner from Aerosoles and MAC is the Theresa Hotel. They don't know. They overlook these things that we see on a regular basis.

KAVON: Yeah, like the way the old Apollo was before the glitzy lights and expensive tickets. You think we [black people] can afford to go there now?

QUENTIN: You mean before all the white people started feeling safe enough to take over Harlem and our community spots? The new Apollo is their new "art space" in what they think is an exotic black neighborhood. That's funny, man!

KAVON: But what other people think is . . . art in Harlem isn't the real of . . . the everyday.

QUENTIN: Not the conditions we have to live in. Why do I have to live in an apartment building with a cheap fire escape when right around the corner is a new building with real balconies for all the new apartments? Why do I have to deal with trash and signs of crime and drugs when they don't have to?

KAVON: Yeah, right across the street from my projects are condos with balconies. Right across the street! It's so different across there. These are the things people don't want to see. They believe that what's going on here in our community is like a second renaissance . . . another Harlem Renaissance.

QUENTIN: A second what . . . Harlem Renaissance? Don't get me wrong, there's a lot of newness in Harlem, some for the good, some for the bad, some I just don't understand yet. But how can the new replace the old: condos versus projects, whites versus blacks, balconies versus fire escapes, silence versus community gatherings, not knowing neighbors versus having people's backs. And this is a renaissance?

KAVON: Clean surroundings versus trash and crime, drugs, funky smells.

QUENTIN: It's an either-or situation we're living in, so to say Harlem is going through a second renaissance ain't right. Don't get me wrong: there's art underneath all this rubble. You just gotta look really hard for it.

Kavon and Quentin's exchange echoes Haymes's articulation (1995) of how a pedagogy of place should be attentive to race and struggle in urban communities. This articulation involves the physical space, material conditions, and changing landscape of Harlem, or the "old versus new." For Kavon and Quentin, this dichotomous relationship includes visual images of community such as the Theresa Hotel, the Schomburg Center, and crowds of people on the streets. It also includes discourses on and assumptions about who or what belongs in Harlem: "white versus blacks," "condos versus projects," "balconies versus fire escapes." When asked to talk about art in Harlem, or as Quentin names it, "Harlem as art," the concern becomes one of belonging in a community undergoing rapid changes associated with gentrification, shifting demographics, and forgotten histories.

Kavon, Quentin, and I documented stories of change through photography, mapping, and video documentaries, beginning with the areas surrounding their home spaces. Kavon's documentation began with a reflexive look at art in his community. He grappled with how to claim art in "the Frederick Douglass Projects when all around me are people who don't care,

New Directions for Adult and Continuing Education • DOI: 10.1002/ace

who throw paper [trash] on the ground, who sell drugs, who just hang out." He added, "I get tired of seeing this. I guess the art's there, since Harlem is a history landmark of African culture and struggle." Nevertheless, Kavon is quick to point out to me the very name of his housing complex, Frederick Douglass, as he directs Quentin to get a video shot of the white-and-black signs that bear this ex-slave's name. Kavon remarks, "When I think of Harlem as art, I gotta look around where I live, to get a better handle of history here. Douglass was a slave and then an abolitionist. That's important for black people to know. That's art through, um, struggle."

As Kavon recognizes signs of history in his community, he also narrates a story of belonging through art forms. With a digital camera, he took pictures of the Frederick Douglass projects, the row of abandoned storefronts adjacent to the projects, and the condominiums with balconies across the street. He then took Quentin and myself on a video walk-through of the area. As he described his negative feelings toward gentrification, he pointed out how creation of newness—new condominiums, new residents, and new businesses that will enter the community—ignores schools, local stores, and housing projects that quickly fall into disrepair. Kavon's visual texts (photographs, video interviews) represent what linguistic modes of communication could not capture: "aesthetically communicative power" (Vasudevan, 2006, p. 14) of a youngster employing art forms to narrate stories of community. His stories are embedded in spatial, or geographical, struggle and contribute to his emerging definition of art.

Much like Kavon, Quentin had a story about art in his immediate surroundings, particularly the art of the new—renovated apartments, balconies, influx of white people—versus the art of the old—old apartments, fire escapes, longtime black residents. Quentin accepted Kavon's acknowledgment of "signs of history" just as much as he related to Kavon's feelings about local sites left in disrepair: "There are projects, abandoned lots, in the center of this new art, and nobody seems to think this is crazy? If nobody stands up to this to show people how Harlem is art, and has been for years, then what's going to be left? Will they take away the Adam Clayton Powell Building 'cause they need that block of space for more high rises?" Quentin continues by talking about the Apollo Theater as a local space where new talents performed on "Amateur Night" and where one could get an inexpensive ticket to see famous acts "do their thing on stage." This is no longer a reality for Quentin, who expresses shock at seeing a long line of white people going into the Apollo on a Wednesday night in May 2006. He comments: "We [Quentin and I] were walking from the Powell Building, just left a meeting where adult activists where complaining about living conditions, increased rent, and unfair conditions by management in their housing complexes. Then next thing I know, we approach the Apollo, and there they are . . . claiming our community art spot as their own. Probably not even realizing that the artwork on the concrete and fenced walls next to the Apollo was created by a local working black artist. I'm glad I had the digital [camera]."

With the camera, Quentin took pictures of "white people in front of the redone Apollo." In our shared rhyme book and in subsequent interview sessions, he compared the pictures to those he took of black people going into the Studio Museum of Harlem, waiting for the bus in front of the Powell building, and of construction sites for new condominiums near where he lives, just eight blocks south of 125th Street. In his comparison, he highlights the race of the "white people in front of the redone Apollo" as an indication of a changing, soon-to-be gentrified community: "They were never here when I was growing up. They were too afraid to come to Harlem, and at night? Never would've happened." In juxtaposition with black people going into the museum or waiting on the bus, Quentin admits that the presence of "lines of white people" in Harlem makes him uncomfortable because "they change the face of this community and take away the real meanings of art in a place like the Apollo. Blacks always been going to the Apollo, to the museum, whether they live in Harlem or just visiting." He continues: "Most blacks know Harlem and live in a similar space. We share that struggle. But whites know Harlem as an artsy place because of gentrification. It's not the same kind of knowing." For Quentin, the connections among race, place, belonging, and struggle are significant.

During his video walk-through, Quentin pointed out the renovated apartment building on one corner, the new drugstore on another, and the "crazy priced" dry cleaners close by. He spoke of an abandoned laundromat in the same breath that he talked about a vacant lot, now barricaded, where many community members met for social events: "This is what I see on the regular. I didn't pay much attention to it before, but now I do. And do I see any art in all this rubble? New condo over here, old apartment building over there! New dry cleaners there, closed laundromat here! Right here in Harlem. Yeah, I have to, if I want to remember history. I believe the old is more of art than the temporary new."

The old, for Quentin, Kavon, and many longtime black residents in the area, including Vivian, Barbara, Thelma, and John, signifies a spatial history of struggle and survival. In this moment, the documented representations of art and community captured by the youngsters influenced adult learning. By engaging in conversation with and explaining their perspective on gentrification to Vivian and the other adults, Quentin and Kavon initiated an inquiry into the value of sharing community stories across age and experience. They encouraged the adults to question current community practices (the value of gatherings and meetings and taking care of and protecting the community) and assumptions (young people have no voice; they do not care about the community). At the same time, the adults encouraged Quentin and Kavon to study the community's long history of struggle (segregation, fights for civil rights) and political leadership (Malcolm X, Adam

C. Powell). In this context, learning became reciprocal, active, and transformational for both the adults and the youngsters. Youth activism was met
with adult learning.

From their encounter with adult residents, Quentin and Kavon spent
the next few weeks examining their pictures and imagining, as Vivian asked
them to do, the untold stories by adults in their community and school of
what was in Harlem. Their imaginings led them to consider how the past—
the "what was here before"—served as precursor to the real Harlem Renaissance and civil rights protests. Vivian's suggestion for Quentin and Kavon
to study Harlem's long history is captured in their many photographs, video
interviews, and conversations, all of which support the youngsters' claim
that "Harlem is art." These artifacts attest to their growing interest in collaborating with adults to document stories and reclaim Harlem from gentrification and commercialization.

Also captured in the material representation of this work are the voices
of two youngsters perplexed by the influx of newness in Harlem: on the one
hand, they are ecstatic to see new chain drugstores but dismayed to no longer
participate in certain community rituals. According to Quentin, "Many stores
in the area have opened, bringing in different people. This changes the whole
feeling of Harlem, including the arts." Kavon agrees, insisting that Harlem
has always been a place where art forms dominate, even on "less than popular neighborhood streets." He claims, "Before new stores, there were the
conversations, museums, parades, festivals, block performances. We don't
have them as much because so many residents have left since they can't
afford to stay. But Harlem is art; gentrification can't take that away." Reiterative of this point are Kavon and Quentin's pictures of the Cotton Club, Studio
Museum, Harlem YMCA, Audubon Ballroom, Abyssinian Baptist Church,
Duke Ellington Statue, and Marcus Garvey Park. Their pictures capture a
legacy of artistic and political action in Harlem and throughout the African
Diaspora. Their images portray art as a vehicle that opened the doors to
African American expression of the Harlem Renaissance.

The pictures speak volumes to their emerging definition of art "as experience" and as visible signs of everyday life. For Quentin and Kavon, the pictures are connected to what they call the 1920s' "youth and adult arts
movement" in Harlem, a movement that saw the likes of African American
literary scholars Langston Hughes, Zora Neale Hurston, and James Weldon
Johnson. It also recognized the value of young artists apprenticing with
adult members of the community, which helped to create Harlem as a major
site for black cultural expression. If anything, the significance of art in
Harlem parallels the community's historical struggle with representation,
racism, and socioeconomic strife. Now that Harlem is undergoing gentrification, one wonders, "Where are the adults, the black residents and political leaders, the people who are supposed to protect the community?
The social activists, the politicians, the teachers, the artists? The people

we are told to follow? Where's everybody, the other Vivians? And where are the apprenticeship models from the Harlem Renaissance?" (Kavon, Quentin, and Valerie).

Conclusions and Implications

KAVON: I look at Harlem and think art is more than writing, poetry, drawing, dancing, and singing.

QUENTIN: Art is also struggle. That's Harlem.

VALERIE: Seems as if we believe the same things about "Harlem as art."

QUENTIN: Yeah, but not too many adults would say that. I don't think too many adults believe people like me and Kavon have anything important to say about art and Harlem. It goes back to something I said before . . . some people think they have the right to talk and others don't. Some think that Harlem is just a lot of poor black people living in projects who don't care about the community.

KAVON: We care, that's why we're doing this project. We know that we have to care. It would be good if adults would accept this. You know, adults can learn a lot from us . . . Vivian did.

VALERIE: Like what?

KAVON: Like the changes happening in Harlem affect hard-working, struggling black people who've been living here for a long time. Young people like Quentin and me know that, we see that, and we're documenting the changes with our cameras. Telling stories that need to be told.

QUENTIN: You [adults] just can't sit around and complain all day long about the changes without listening to what other people got to say. And we are a part of those other people. Adults need to know that young people in Harlem can do something about the changes . . . by staying focused on life and getting their voice out there. More adults should recognize that youngsters want a better future and know the changes that need to be made are: less violence, more education, better leaders.

KAVON: Clean and safe communities! These all have to do with Harlem as art.

VALERIE: So, Harlem is art in the sense that it has all of the traditional art forms—museums, entertainment venues, lovely architecture, a strong literary history, festivals, the history of the Harlem Renaissance and the artists who came with that period. But if I am hearing you right, Quentin and Kavon, "Harlem as art" encompasses human struggles with place and race, what you call "rubble," Quentin. Is this right?

QUENTIN: That's right. And the rubble is the sounds of the 'hood, the people, the struggle, our whole history. That's the rubble; that's the art . . . the experiences.

VALERIE: I think adults can learn a lot from this work.

KAVON: We know. We know. You think they know?

Quentin and Kavon are aware of the distance between adult and youth efforts to document art forms in Harlem. They understand that such distance oftentimes results from conflicting perspectives, ways of knowing, and struggles that hinder the emergence of intergroup relations and democratic engagement. There is tension around who should represent the *truths* of a changing Harlem and who has the right to speak. This tension exists between youths and adults, but it also transcends age groups to include race. Quentin's assertion about "white people in front of the redone Apollo" and Kavon's belief that "what other people think is . . . art in Harlem isn't the real of . . . the everyday" illustrate their awareness and discomfort with signs of otherness. Underneath their observations are serious concerns for adults to attend to: examining how Harlem as art is a call for people of various ages and races to coexist across imaginary, physical, and cultural boundaries; imagining how art in Harlem can serve as a vehicle that connects groups of people to one another; and negotiating power in Harlem by discussing how the politics of space affects forms of life for youngsters and adults. These are some of the implications of this study on adult learning.

For Quentin and Kavon, Harlem is important and has a major impact on their attitude toward change, activism, and the arts. Where they live has everything to do with how they interpret struggle and identify with life. For this project, their interpretation of struggle is connected to their emerging definition of art as experience as well as to their awareness of the value of the Harlem Renaissance for youths, adults, and location. More important, their work is a gesture to adults in the larger community to reconceptualize activism and the arts by being attentive to the existing differences in and approaches to learning from the art and culture of Harlem. They want to have conversation with adults to find additional ways to document art forms, call attention to ongoing activist efforts, and narrate stories of struggle and survival in the community. They want what adults want: a safe community, clean streets, political activities, socially transformative action (Haymes, 1995), and a call against "normalization" of community (Foucault, 1984). These things can happen through the arts. Harlem is art in this postmodern, postindustrial neighborhood undergoing the reproduction of space. In the words of eighteen-year-old Kavon, "Adults can learn a lot from us."

In learning "a lot from us," this study has taught me that as an adult committed to preserving Harlem's history I must take responsibility for the stories of community and struggle that I share. I, as well as other adults, should better value civic participation, create counternarratives to negative portrayals of urban community, collaboratively inquire into the historical signs that make a community artful, increase our level of activism, and establish apprenticeship models for other adults and youngsters. Doing these things can enhance adult learning and draw positive attention to lived realities of young people in urban communities.

New Directions for Adult and Continuing Education • DOI: 10.1002/ace

References

Beauregard, R. *Voices of Decline: The Postwar Fate of US Cities.* Oxford, UK: Blackwell, 1993.

Castells, M. *The City and the Grassroots.* Berkeley: University of California Press, 1983.

Clark, K. *Dark Ghetto: Dilemmas of Social Power.* New York: HarperCollins, 1965.

Dewey, J. *Art as Experience.* New York: Perigee Trade, 1959.

Foucault, M. "The Means of Correct Training." Translated by R. Howard. In P. Rabinow (ed.), *The Foucault Reader.* New York: Pantheon Books, 1984.

Freire, P. *Pedagogy of the Oppressed.* New York: Continuum, 1995. (Original work published in 1970)

Freire, A.M.A., and Macedo, D. (eds.). *The Paulo Freire Reader.* New York: Continuum, 1998.

Giroux, H. *Border Crossings: Cultural Workers and the Politics of Education.* New York: Routledge, 1992.

Giroux, H. "Living Dangerously: Identity Politics and the New Cultural Racism." In H. Giroux and P. McLaren (eds.), *Between Borders: Pedagogy and the Politics of Cultural Studies.* New York: Routledge, 1994.

Haymes, S. *Race, Culture, and the City: A Pedagogy for Black Urban Struggle.* Albany: State University of New York Press, 1995.

Keith, M., and Pile, S. *Place and the Politics of Identity.* New York: Routledge, 1993.

Lincoln, Y. S., and Guba, E. "Paradigmatic Controversies, Contradictions, and Emerging Confluences." In N. K. Deszin and Y. S. Lincoln (eds.), *Handbook of Qualitative Research* (2nd ed.). Thousand Oaks, Calif.: Sage, 2000.

McLaren, P. "Border Disputes: Multicultural Narrative, Identity Formation, and Critical Pedagogy in Postmodern America." In D. McLaughlin and W. Tierney (eds.), *Naming Silenced Lives: Personal Narratives and the Processes of Educational Change.* New York: Routledge, 1993.

McLaren, P. "Multiculturalism and the Postmodern Critique: Toward a Pedagogy of Resistance and Transformation." In H. Giroux and P. McLaren (eds.), *Between Borders: Pedagogy and the Politics of Cultural Studies.* New York: Routledge, 1994.

Soja, E. *Postmodern Geographies: The Reassertion of Space in Critical Social Theory.* London: Verso, 1990.

Vasudevan, L. "Making Known Differently: Engaging Visual Modalities as Spaces to Author New Selves." *E-Learning,* 2006, 3(2), 207–216.

Wilson, W. J. *The Truly Disadvantaged: The Inner City, the Underclass, and Public Policy.* Chicago: University of Chicago Press, 1987.

VALERIE KINLOCH is assistant professor of adolescent literacy in the School of Teaching and Learning: College of Education and Human Ecology at The Ohio State University.

5

This chapter presents a case study of collaboration between the Lawndale Christian Development Corporation and the Chicago Arts Partnerships in Education.

The Arts as an Occasion for Collective Adult Learning as Authentic Community Development

Arnold Aprill, Richard Townsell

All too often, a community undergoing a community development process is relegated to the role of audience to outsiders' expertise. Community members are asked to furnish token "representation" of the residents' point of view and once they've been represented are asked to approve what the outsiders say is in their best interest. This dynamic is reinforced by whatever power struggles and multiplicity of points of view actually exist inside the community itself, inviting outside experts to create oversimplified, monolithic characterization of the community's wants and needs as a way of responding to the overwhelming number of apparently competing agendas represented by the individual community members themselves. So how is consensus built across differences in age, class, ethnic identity, gender, lifestyles, religion, mobility, language, and values? This chapter presents a case study of the arts as an occasion for collective adult learning as authentic community development, as seen in a collaboration between the Lawndale Christian Development Corporation (LCDC) and the Chicago Arts Partnerships in Education (CAPE).

Community Development as a Process of Collective Adult Learning

One way to build consensus across difference is to see the community development process *as a collective adult learning process itself*. Building

NEW DIRECTIONS FOR ADULT AND CONTINUING EDUCATION, no. 116, Winter 2007 © 2007 Wiley Periodicals, Inc.
Published online in Wiley InterScience (www.interscience.wiley.com) • DOI: 10.1002/ace.276

new housing is not just about bricks and mortar but also about developing new collective understanding of where and how we live. School improvement is not just about hiring and firing principals but also about developing new collective understanding of the community's relationship to its schools. Economic development is not just about jobs and businesses but also about developing new collective understanding of the intentional design of a neighborhood's cultural ecology. Parks and recreation are not just about planting trees and building a movie theater but also about developing new collective understanding of our relationship to the natural world in urban settings, and to our needs for relaxation, pleasure, and entertainment.

A collective adult learning framework is meaningful and useful in this context, because collective adult learning *actually invites and benefits* from the dialectical nature of differing opinions and experiences. A learning process that can tolerate and encourage opposing subjectivities affords the kind of respect and listening that is a precondition for reflection and dialogue (Mezirow, 1991, 2000; Daloz, 2000)—which are also the preconditions for developing consensus, for planning, and for collective action (Marsick, Bitterman, and van der Veen, 2000).

A collective adult learning framework moves participants involved with community development planning from individuals defending a position to learners reframing ideas by hearing interesting ideas that challenge their assumptions in a generative way. There are significant parallels here to the adult learning literature on team learning, where there is movement from fragmented individual learning to pooled and synergistic learning (Kasl, Marsick, and Dechant, 1997). Individuals enter a conversation regarding their community as individuals and leave with a common understanding of an issue. They leave with a fundamentally different interpretation of the situation; they have contributed to reframing the issues, and they have also reframed it for themselves.

A collective adult learning framework addresses issues of scale by including significant and diverse portions of the community (Daloz, 2000). When a large number of community residents see themselves as deepening their learning about themselves and their community by working in a learning context with others, they can move much more quickly into a collective problem-solving mode that is respectful of others and that does not reduce their experiential knowledge to tokenism. Challenging ideas that expand rather than discount lived experience are gratifying in themselves. This becomes an engine for building consensus. A *collective adult learning* framework recognizes both young adults and elders, two constituencies who are often patronized and discounted in the community development process as less than full contributors to collective knowledge.

How the Arts Assist the Collective Adult Learning Process

For collective adult learning to become reflective and generative, experience, knowledge, intuition, and insights of all participating learners need to be revealed both to the learners themselves *and* to other learners. The arts, as especially rich and varied media for revealing experience, knowledge, intuition, and insight, have special power for accelerating the reflective dialogue at the heart of collective adult learning (Davis-Manigaulte, Yorks, and Kasl, 2006; Yorks and Kasl, 2006). Our collaboration was facilitated by our participation in a cooperative inquiry that was part of the Leadership for a Changing World awardees program funded by the Ford Foundation and the Advocacy Institute and was administered through the Research Center for Leadership in Action at NYU's Wagner School (Aprill and others, 2006). During our inquiry, we discussed the radical epistemology of John Heron and Peter Reason (Heron, 1992; Heron and Reason, 1997, 2001). Heron and Reason's epistemological framework involves four ways of knowing: *experiential* (involving "direct face-to-face encounter with person, place, or thing . . . knowing through the immediacy of perceiving through empathy and resonance"), *presentational* ("the first form of expressing meaning and significance through drawing on expressive forms of imagery through . . . music drawing, painting, . . . story, . . . and so on"), *propositional* (knowing "about something through . . . theories, expressed in informative statements"), and *practical* ("how to do something . . . expressed through skill, knack, or competence" (2001, p. 183). At the level of individual learning, presentational or expressive learning is a pathway between experiential knowing and structured propositional knowing. As such it opens a connection between emotion and feeling and critical reflection. At the interpersonal and group level presentational, or expressive, knowing permits an empathic connection between individuals and is a pathway for critical discourse (Yorks and Kasl, 2006; see Figure 5.1). This empathic connection is the basis for learning-within-relationship amid diversity (Yorks and Kasl, 2002).

Building on these ideas, we used art as a core component of collaborative community development work on certain principles of collective adult learning:

• *Revealing the learner's knowledge to the learner.* All learners are full of images, ideas, impulses, and intuitions that are preverbal and emergent but unformed. The structures of the several arts disciplines give expressive shape to these messages, so that the learner can know what he or she knows but has not yet expressed and bring this knowledge to consciousness as well as out into the world.

• *Revealing the learner's knowledge to others.* The arts literally present an image of another person's consciousness that other learners can respond

Figure 5.1. Expressive Knowing Is A Pathway

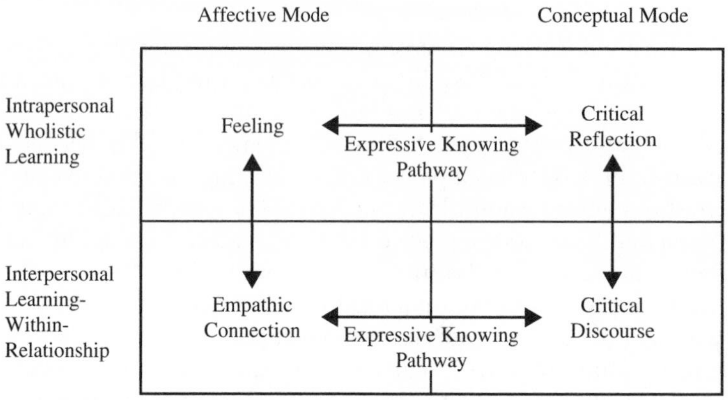

Affective Mode   Conceptual Mode

Intrapersonal Wholistic Learning	Feeling ⟵⟶ Expressive Knowing Pathway	Critical Reflection
Interpersonal Learning-Within-Relationship	Empathic Connection ⟵⟶ Expressive Knowing Pathway	Critical Discourse

Source: Reprinted from Yorks and Kasl (2006). Reprinted by permission of the author and Sage Communications, Inc.; from Journal of Transformative Education (4)1.

to in their own way, allowing a multifaceted entry point into another learner's thinking—expanding, reframing, and enriching everyone's thinking. Once revealed, this knowledge needs enough "independence" from the learner from whom it was generated to become shared knowledge, to become a "proposition" owned and considered by all the members of the learning team. Arts products establish this distance by first emerging as expression of their individual creators, but then also having independent "lives" of their own that resonate with and evoke new experience and expression from others. The richness and variation in response that arts products stimulate in a group of learners both bonds the group and generates new thinking among individuals and the collective. Concrete examples of this process are given in the case study of this chapter.

LCDC Disengages Itself from the Horns of a Dilemma

Leadership of the Lawndale Christian Development Corporation (LCDC) was in the process of figuring out how to work with LISC (Local Initiatives Support Corporation) Chicago, a nationally known community development intermediary. LISC had chosen sixteen Chicago neighborhoods to work on a ten-year planning and implementation process for creation of quality-of-life plans for those neighborhoods. This work was largely funded by the MacArthur Foundation. LISC and LCDC were both struggling to clarify their roles in the Lawndale community development planning process. The LCDC leadership thought that CAPE (a network of schools and arts organizations that codesign and coimplement innovative school improvement strategies) might be useful in destabilizing some of the competition for the platform in planning with the Lawndale community.

CAPE introduced a lateral intervention: an art-based community visioning process that was helpful in reinforcing some of LCDC's core principles while leaving LISC an opportunity to bring its assets to the table without discounting LCDC's history and practice.

CAPE as a Collective Adult Education Network

All of CAPE's work in schools and communities is based on a collective adult education model (www.capeweb.org). Many arts education organizations deliver arts services to the classroom, in which visiting artists offer a short-term series of arts activities for students while the teacher is often relegated to the role of disciplinarian. Many teachers choose to "walk" while visiting artists carry out lessons, grading papers at the back of the room or slipping out to smoke a cigarette. Teachers are not engaged in the arts learning in their classrooms because they are not engaged as learners themselves. The visiting artists often fall into the trap of presenting charming but superficial lessons that expose children to art but do not engage the students as complex thinkers making their own decisions about problems that matter. This is sometimes referred to as "art as inoculation." The artists are also not engaged as learners, coming into the school community as experts rather than colearners.

CAPE challenges this delivery model by positing a capacity-building, colearning model, gathering teachers and artists into an adult learning community that codesigns innovative programming in schools and investigates and documents effective teaching, learning, and art making across schools. The Collaborative Cut-Paper Mural Process described here embodies CAPE's values of shared learning through collective work.

The Collaborative Cut-Paper Mural Process. The noted African American artist Bernard Williams (http://cuip.uchicago.edu/ac/Artists/BWilliams/) developed the visioning process that CAPE introduced to the Lawndale community.

Williams's work grows from his continuing investigation of American and world history and culture. As the artist notes, "In many of my works, signs and symbols are collected and arranged in order to speak about the complexities of history and human development and movement through the ages. I attempt to speak about America as a place of conflict, sharing, fragmentation, and convergence. America is seen as a place constructed by multiple cultures, including Anglos, Hispanics, Blacks, Asians, and others. The viewer is urged to consider his or her place in the forceful flow of culture and events."

Williams's rich and varied works often contain simple, iconographic, silhouetted images forming symbols that resonate with multiple meanings beyond their simple outlines (Figure 5.2). His process includes:

1. Collecting lots of information about complex subjects that matter to people's lives (acknowledging complexity)

New Directions for Adult and Continuing Education • DOI: 10.1002/ace

Figure 5.2. Bernard Williams with Collaborative Cut-Paper Mural About the Great Migration

Note: Photo by Arnold Aprill.

2. Developing simple images that stand for complex ideas (representing complexity)
3. Arranging these simple images into patterns (exploring complexity)
4. Reflecting on the patterns in the arrangement (analyzing complexity)

Under Williams's guidance, CAPE has used this process as a teaching methodology to allow groups to develop collective understanding of complex subjects. In CAPE projects using this technique, groups write down a list of important ideas and images from a subject that matters to them, individuals draw simple images representing these ideas on construction paper and cut them out, the images are arranged into a mural and taped to a wall or large sheet of paper for all to see, and then the group analyzes patterns they see in the arrangement. The results are consistently beautiful, are inclusive of multiple points of view, and produce lively discussion and analysis among all the participants. It is literally a visioning process because it translates ideas into images one can see, allowing viewers some distance on the ideas and the opportunity to consider how the ideas interact with each other to suggest new options. CAPE first used this process as part of its Great Migration Project, in which CAPE teachers and artists traveled to the Mississippi Delta to meet with teachers and artists from Mississippi to collectively grapple with the complex history of African American migration from Mississippi to Chicago.

A Light Bulb Goes on for Richard Townsell. The initial experience of the arts during one of Arnie's activities in the Leadership for a Changing World (LCW) program initially created a disorienting dilemma for Richard that through reflection led to a new insight regarding the potential of the arts for his work in community development.

> At the start of the LCW meeting, Arnold Aprill led us in the cut-paper mural process. I was skeptical, along with other hard-scrabble community organizers from around the country. We are going to cut out paper and make a mural, I thought. What have I gotten myself into? Arnold asked us to cut out pictures or words that described our hopes and our fears about leadership. People were self-conscious about their art, and Arnold assured us that we were not going to put it up in a museum.
>
> Slowly we began to stick up our work up on the wall. I had a lot of fun doing the pieces that I put up. I immediately thought that this process could be used in the community, as we were engaging in a comprehensive planning process for the next ten years for our neighborhood. I saw the arts as an invaluable tool in helping the community create a vision about its future. The more I thought about it, the more I realized that the arts could serve as a democratizing tool to level the playing field between experts and novices [Richard Townsell, in Aprill and others, 2006].

Richard came to the realization that although LCDC had created award-winning housing and even produced some murals, the arts could become more than an afterthought, a decoration after the fact in Lawndale's development process. The arts could become part of his community's learning process. He saw that the role of the arts in community development has been largely relegated to art activities and products such as mosaics, sculptures, and single performances. Those activities are useful, but he began to wonder how the arts could be instrumental in the methodology of community development planning, rather than just ancillary products to community development. He decided to try it out.

Making Cut-Paper Murals in Lawndale. Richard invited Arnold to introduce the cut-paper mural process into Lawndale's first large planning meeting. The LISC team was very skeptical, requesting repeated phone meetings in which Arnold patiently repeated the same information each time, understanding that the process sounded ridiculous until it was experienced.

Richard's team intentionally invited a large group of participants (two hundred people), recognizing that the process, by going back and forth among individual work, small group work, and whole group work, could effectively engage large groups. Rather than winnowing this group down to a small set of decision makers, LCDC values inclusion of a broad base of community members in every aspect of the community development process. LCDC also consistently and persistently goes back to dropouts and nonparticipants to investigate what the obstacles are to their authentic inclusion.

The steps in the collaborative cut-paper mural development process (writing down important ideas in small groups, creating individual images, arranging the individual images into collective images, and discussing the patterns that emerge) work together to form a positive dynamic between individual expression and collective decision making, and they are concrete demonstrations of relationship building.

- *Step one: collecting information, acknowledging complexity.* After welcomes and food, the group was introduced to the process and shown slides of cut-paper murals created by other planning groups. During the initial presentation of the mural process to the Lawndale community, a piece of music was played as an exemplar of grassroots art making. It was composed that very morning as an online collaboration between grade school students in Chicago and students in Australia and emailed to CAPE that afternoon. A young man stepped forward in a state of pleased shock. He had made up part of the American end of that transcontinental collaboration. He was transformed, almost before he realized what he had accomplished, into an international artist being held up as a model for his whole community, with his mother as a witness. But that was not all. He was immediately drafted to be the videographer for the evening, and he engaged a buddy of his to become the digital still photographer. The equipment was unfamiliar to them, but they mastered both cameras in a few minutes and fulfilled their new roles with gusto.

The group then broke up into tables by areas of interest in community planning. Table topics included education; arts, recreation, and culture; economic development and jobs; health and safety; affordable housing; and youth development. There, working in small groups, very mixed tables brainstormed images of what they would like to see in the community in their topic area. One elderly lady reported on a long-closed neighborhood bakery she fondly remembered from her youth. "Mostly I remember the smell of fresh baked bread," she said. "And how I'd love to see a bakery that served good tea and coffee!" One parent spoke of her longing for not just competent schools in the neighborhood but schools of choice for learners from other neighborhoods. A young person spoke of the need for more after-school programs in the neighborhood. At every table, all ideas were recorded, in all their variety.

This brainstorming returns the community planning process to its true purpose, which is planning rather than the competitive distraction of slicing up the fiscal pie of grants.

• *Step two: developing images, representing complexity.* The groups, working at their tables, were then directed to draw and cut out simple images representing their brainstormed ideas, drawing outlines with pencil before cutting. Participants were also encouraged to include key words as images to be cut out. Participants were assured that "talent" was not required, that even very simple images look great. The familiar materials involved in the process (pencils, paper, scissors, masking tape) and the seemingly simple tasks (write some words, draw a simple outline, cut it out, tape it up) made for inviting access to the art-making process.

• *Step three: arranging images into patterns, exploring complexity.* Participants were then directed to arrange their images into a collective mural at each table, attaching images with masking tape so that images can be moved, shifted, and rearranged. Each table negotiated the collective arrangement of individual images. Contradictory images (such as alcohol and healthy food) were both included. Each image was ripe for interpretation as patterns began to emerge from the collective arrangements. Symbols represent complex ideas in simple ways, retaining latent complexity that is revealed through interpretation.

• *Step four: reflecting on patterns, analyzing complexity.* Working at each table, participants identified the themes that emerged from the juxtaposition of diverse images and then chose representatives from each table to present emergent themes to the entire group. In the cut-paper mural process, all people present in the room participate, regardless of age, income, or expertise. The facilitators make certain that everyone has an opportunity to participate, and that no one monopolizes the conversation. In the LCDC planning sessions, children and senior citizens took the floor with equal dignity, both having valuable contributions to make from their own experience about what was needed in their shared community. The democratizing nature of the activity (one artistic vote per person in mural creation) allows nay-sayers to have their nay-say without controlling the conversation with their negativity, as well as for diverse problem solvers to reframe the conversation in useful new ways. For example, under the topic of recreation one Lawndale resident added the image of a bookstore, noting the absence of one in the neighborhood. This was an important new insight that could easily have been left out of community planning.

In the reflection step of the mural process, the community is called on to report how each piece of the mural speaks meaningfully to other pieces and to other people. Everyone appreciates having his or her contribution to the whole acknowledged and valued. Communities grow by realizing the gifts of neighbors.

• *Step five: Taking time.* This gratifying activity helped the group pause for planning. One of the biggest difficulties in community development is setting aside the appropriate time for planning, and for monitoring when time is wasted and when it is well spent. There are two constituencies that tend to accelerate the process: outside planners, who confuse efficiency with effectiveness, and community members, highly skeptical of initiatives that have proven in the past to be time-burners masking a hidden agenda and understandably impatient for results. The impulse is to try to go faster, whether speed is called for or not. The mural process helps concretize the essential time needed for visioning, yielding satisfying public evidence that something has been accomplished even in early planning, and also creating a reference point for looking back on early decisions.

Reflecting on the Process: Values and Principles

Looking back on their collaboration, we reflected on the LCDC values the organizations had held to during the process, and the parallel community arts principles they had enacted.

• *LCDC value:* community development is more about building relationships than it is about building buildings. *The arts-as-community-development principle:* the person-to-person discourse at the center of the process produces murals that represent groups of people in discussion with each other, rather than murals that represent the vision of a single outside art expert. This parallels LCDC's commitment to decisions emerging out of community discourse rather than from the thinking of outside experts. Also, the commitment to art as an inclusive process (not a focus on art as attractive artifact) models LCDC's belief that relationships build buildings better than buildings build relationships.

• *LCDC value:* community development is about diverse participation across barriers of race, class, gender, and age. *The arts-as-community-development principle:* democratic culture depends on every voice speaking out. The arts quite literally lift every voice.

• *LCDC value:* community development is about inclusive and broad participation. *The arts-as-community-development principle:* the arts assist democratic discourse across large groups of people.

• *LCDC value:* community development planning processes need to be transparent to the communities involved. *The arts-as-community-development principle:* art-making processes that invite broad participation support local decision making, reveal process through participation, and thereby demystify expertise.

• *LCDC value:* community development takes the time it takes to develop communities, rather than the time dictated by grant schedules. *The arts-as-community-development principle:* The arts help focus attention on key early planning decisions and produce compelling evidence of key decisions to help guide the tempo of and benchmarks for later decision making.

• *LCDC value:* community development places more value on developing ideas than on dividing up money. *The arts-as-community-development principle:* community arts practice keeps our eyes on the prize of meaning, not money. The arts can make explicit and visible our true values and deep motivations, which then assists us in prioritizing appropriate and fair use and distribution of dollars and other resources as means to worthy ends.

• *LCDC value:* community development encourages community members to assume new roles and investigate new capacities. *The arts-as-community-development principle:* literally put technology and responsibility into the hands of community members, especially those that have not had opportunities to lead. People grow into the challenges afforded them. They rise. Encourage collaborators to shift roles; the documenter becomes the reporter, the student becomes the teacher, the teacher becomes the artist. Comfort with role migration is a strong indicator of successful community development.

• *LCDC value:* community development recognizes all contributors. *The arts-as-community-development principle:* The arts assist community members in seeing tangibly each other's and one's own contributions to collective tasks.

• *LCDC value:* community development distributes leadership rather than centralizing it. *The arts-as-community-development principle:* the mural process focuses the community on the beauty of its collective work, rather than on the ego of a few leaders. Community arts practice builds the capacity of all, rather than idealizing the accomplishments of the few. Also, the shared meeting ground of distributed leadership prepares the current generation of leadership to step out of the way and pass leadership on to the next generation, preparing that generation to receive its responsibility and power.

• *LCDC value:* community development recognizes community members as authors of their own destiny. *The arts-as-community-development principle:* community arts practice recognizes community members as not just consumers of culture but creators of culture.

• *LCDC value:* community development deals with harsh realities but is essentially a spiritual practice. *The arts-as-community-development principle:* the mural process, with its shared image making, communal testifying, and reflection, creates communion in community.

Conclusion

The arts can build particular capacities among adult learners in the community development process. Communities engaged in community planning are often directed by experts to look at outsiders' plans for building new housing and retail opportunities. Including an artistic point of view in the planning process itself redirects community members to create their own vision for their community, drawing on their lived knowledge as adult thinkers responsible for their own destinies. This redirected energy leads to activism. The arts encourage all community members to speak out and be heard, and to connect vision to action. Creating artistic products during the planning process contributes to a sense of agency, emboldening citizens to determine new actions for themselves and their community.

Weaving a communal art process into LCDC's community development planning helped move Lawndale residents into a shared "state of grace" in which they spoke to each other with deepened strength, vision, and commitment and listened to each other with deepened respect, appreciation, and joy. If community-based planning and development is to have any meaningful political power or significant personal value, we need to move ourselves—now—into the spiritual state we want our communities to embody in the future. The arts are a powerful road less taken on this essential journey.

References

Aprill, A., Holliday, E., Jeffers, F., Miyamoto, N., Scher, A., Spatz, D., Townsell, R., Yeh, L., Yorks, L., and Hayes, S. *Can the Arts Change the World? The Transformative Power of the Arts in Fostering and Sustaining Social Change: A Leadership for a Changing World Cooperative Inquiry.* Leadership for a Changing World Program, Research and Documentation Component. New York: Research Center for Leadership in Action, Robert F. Wagner Graduate School of Public Service, New York University, 2006.

Daloz, L.A.P. "Transformative Learning for the Common Good." In J. Mezirow (ed.), *Learning as Transformation: Critical Perspectives on a Theory in Progress.* San Francisco: Jossey-Bass, 2000.

Davis-Manigaulte, J., Yorks, L., and Kasl, E. "Presentational Knowing and Transformative Learning." In E. W. Taylor (ed.), *Fostering Transformative Learning in the Classroom: Challenges and Innovations.* New Directions for Adult and Continuing Education, no. 109. San Francisco: Jossey-Bass, 2006.

Heron, J. *Feeling and Personhood: Psychology in Another Key.* Thousand Oaks, Calif.: Sage, 1992.

Heron, J., and Reason, P. "A Participatory Inquiry Paradigm." *Qualitative Inquiry,* 1997, 3, 274–294.

Heron, J., and Reason, P. "The Practice of Cooperative Inquiry." In P. Reason and H. Bradbury (eds.), *Handbook of Action Research: Participative Inquiry and Practice.* Thousand Oaks, Calif.: Sage, 2001.

Kasl, E., Marsick, V. J., and Dechant, K. "Teams as Learners: A Research-Based Model of Team Learning." *Journal of Applied Behavioral Science,* 1997, 33, 227–246.

Marsick, V. J., Bitterman, J., and van der Veen, R. *From the Learning Organization to Learning Communities: Toward a Learning Society.* Information Series no. 382. Columbus, Ohio: ERIC Clearinghouse, 2000.

Mezirow, J. *Transformative Dimensions of Adult Learning.* San Francisco: Jossey-Bass, 1991.

Mezirow, J. "Learning to Think Like an Adult: Core Concepts of Transformation Theory." In J. Mezirow (ed.), *Learning as Transformation: Critical Perspectives on a Theory in Progress.* San Francisco: Jossey-Bass, 2000.

Yorks, L., and Kasl, E. "Toward a Theory and Practice for Whole-Person Learning: Reconceptualizing Experience and the Role of Affect." *Adult Education Quarterly*, 2002, 52, 176–192.

Yorks, L., and Kasl, E. "I Know More Than I Can Say: A Taxonomy for Utilizing Expressive Ways of Knowing to Foster Transformative Learning." *Journal of Transformative Education*, 2006, 4(1), 1–22.

ARNOLD APRILL *is the executive director of the Chicago Arts Partnerships in Education (CAPE), a network of public schools and artists and arts organizations committed to school improvement through arts education partnerships.*

RICHARD TOWNSELL *is one of seventeen national recipients of the 2003 Ford Foundation's Leadership for a Changing World Award, honoring those who make a difference in their communities by tackling tough social problems.*

6

This chapter looks at the power of theater and literature programs to affect correctional facilities; it delves into how such programs can deepen connections to oneself, to others, to community, and to the larger world.

Texts as Teachers: Shakespeare Behind Bars and Changing Lives Through Literature

Jean Trounstine

Growing up, I never imagined the world of women behind bars. Like most Americans, I thought of criminals as people who deserved to be punished and left it at that. But from an early age, I was interested in theater, literature, and writing, and fascinated with the characters I met in books—characters with the power to influence who I might become. So it wasn't surprising that when the sixties arrived and my Midwestern horizons were blown apart as assumptions about America began to crumble, I found myself a struggling actress in the San Francisco Bay Area, in the audience of Rick Cluchey's *The Cage,* a play performed by ex-prisoners from San Quentin.

Cluchey had botched a bank robbery and been sentenced to San Quentin in the 1950s for life without parole (Kaltenhauser, 1999). After seeing a famed prison production of *Waiting for Godot,* he took to playwriting. While the country sent soldiers to war, Cluchey wrote about another kind of horror. He called it *Le Cage,* setting his play in a French prison so he wouldn't upset San Quentin's administration. I remember the shock of seeing the production, the epiphany that occurred to me. The image of artists in prison—depicted as a cage crowded with men who were shaking their bars in rage—stuck in my mind. Cluchey had found something that no prison could deny him, something no school could teach. Creating art behind bars was a means of survival, a call to arms. For as much as Cluchey and the performers experienced transformation, so, I wagered, did every

NEW DIRECTIONS FOR ADULT AND CONTINUING EDUCATION, no. 116, Winter 2007 © 2007 Wiley Periodicals, Inc.
Published online in Wiley InterScience (www.interscience.wiley.com) • DOI: 10.1002/ace.277

person who saw that play. I could never claim naïveté about the prison system again.

At the time, theater was bursting with experimental approaches, appealing to those of us estranged from societal norms. Jerzy Grotowski's *Towards a Poor Theatre* (1970) spoke to taking the lessons of acting into one's deepest self. Grotowski said that the best actors "come to test themselves in something very definite that reaches beyond the meaning of 'theatre' and is more like an act of living and way of existence" (p. 211). Grotowski recognized that the demands of everyday life deadened a person, and that special theater techniques could open up performers and connect them more directly to themselves and their audiences.

I'd spent a summer at Carl Rogers's Center for the Studies of the Person, where I ran a workshop using such theater exercises for self-awareness. I found myself gravitating to the idea of teaching. Rogers, founder of "client-centered" therapy and influenced by the Humanistic Therapy movement, was known for his view that experiential learning paves the road to personal change and growth. This rang true from what I had felt while performing in Grotowski-inspired ensembles and watching the prisoners. Rogers (1969) said that "anything that can be taught to another is relatively inconsequential and has little or no significant influence on behavior." I wondered if this were true. Yes, major lessons seemed to come from the experiential, but if nothing important could really be taught, what then was the point of teaching? How did "significant" change occur? Were the prisoners able to take something from their theater experience into everyday life outside prison? How did that happen? What was that something?

I began to think more about learning, wanting to use my drama degree to actually facilitate change. I wanted to use theater not only as a means of self-expression or as a vehicle for deeper reflection but as a way out of trapped lives. I had no idea what this really meant.

Like many teacher-activists, I started out with a wing and a prayer. I worked first with high school girls who were not able to function in a regular high school. These students would come back from a weekend at home with knives in their laundry bags; they'd hitchhike late at night, pick up strange men who might offer them drugs or sex. They seemed in permanent despair and I felt the tug to give them hope.

Although I knew little of Paulo Freire at this time, Freire (1994) talks extensively about the role of hope in *The Pedagogy of Hope*. He says that for a liberating educational process to occur, both teacher and students must gain a degree of hope through their work together. This notion that both teacher and student must be engaged as learning partners set the stage.

What gave me most satisfaction with my supposedly special ed students came in small moments where I felt a partnership with them. It was hopeful for both student and teacher when I found a text that would touch them. Helen Keller's struggle to learn in *The Miracle Worker* gave perspective to the girls' difficulties; *The Raisin in the Sun* allowed us to talk about fear and racism. Working with these young women who refused to be "taught" by any traditional means led to the realization that the text can be the teacher. Literature can reach deep into the psyche; this was something I had implicitly known as a girl but not understood explicitly as an adult.

There was no way to dictate learning to these girls. They demanded something that mattered to them and a way to engage their attention. I had to become a facilitator. Although Rogers uses the term *facilitator* when he speaks (1969) of his theory of good teaching—one who assists but does not dominate in the classroom—I took my understandings from theater. I saw myself as "the Joker," what famed theater provocateur Augusto Boal (1979) aptly calls his directorial self when he speaks about encouraging actors in scenic development. I spent time in two workshops with Boal himself, one in Toronto and one in New York City, learning this concept. Boal, a close friend of Freire's, advocates a nonauthoritative role for a director, stressing that the theatrical process needs a neutral party to be at its center. The image of someone who has a sense of perspective, a witty way of providing insight without dominating, appealed to me. The light touch or the suggestion got more than the authoritative commandment. The seeds of my work behind bars were sown.

Going Behind Bars

When the job offer came to work at Framingham in 1986, I was teaching in a wealthy suburban high school. The students enlightened me on their own brand of pressures. They worried about getting into college and being accepted; they struggled to differentiate themselves from their parents. They felt afraid they'd never succeed. *Romeo and Juliet* spoke to the intense romantic love many clung to as a way out of their sheltered lives; Elie Wiesel's stunning book of the Holocaust, *Night*, taught them that what they had to fear in themselves was indifference. Although they came from privileged homes, they had their own challenges. I realized that if I took the job to teach behind bars, I'd have an interesting mix of two worlds: hard-working students from the 'burbs and hard-core criminals. In spite of *Le Cage,* I certainly was as beset as my students with clichés from TV that paint the portrait of sexual deviants or endless excitement in a women's prison. I hoped we all might begin to answer the question I still found rumbling inside me: What is it in learning that can lead to real change?

From the beginning, I did not believe education behind bars was to reform the women—that is, to enlighten them about what society says is the "best" way to be, to teach socially accepted behavior as an antidote to crime. I saw conformity as politically driven and often as action without conscience. The prison administration offered two hours of "training"—a polemic insisting inmates were cons who might trick volunteers—noting that the worst practitioners were those who tried to get "too close." How prisoners were indoctrinated I wasn't sure yet, but I distrusted the idea of "correction." Prison education looked at the classroom as a place dedicated to "the high and holy purpose of forming a right character" (Neill, 2006, p. 284); I thought correctional institutions as problematic as those they sought to correct.

The first class of my ten years included Dolly, a white fiftyish grand-mother who brought her knitting to school and started a battered women's group behind bars. She came warily into Program Room Two, which is described in *Shakespeare Behind Bars: The Power of Drama in a Women's Prison* (Trounstine, 2001) as a lonely and overly painted gray-white room with a window half-filled with bars. A piece of track lighting hung from the ceiling. Women sat around a table that had one leg shorter than the other, in metal chairs, and sneaked cigarettes, puffing smoke-rings out the window. Dolly was an obvious maternal type for some of the younger women who called her "Ma." She wrote poems to stay afloat, ones that talked about her brother Eddie and others longing for the things she missed outside: lemons, her grand-daughter, going to her mother's funeral. She had been a hairdresser in "the free world," but she wanted to take college classes, at first to get back at the state for taking away her freedom but eventually because she wanted to expand her horizons. Dolly, who was at the scene but didn't raise a hand to harm the man her lover killed, wrote an eight-page letter protesting her fifteen-years-to-life on the theory of joint venture; she was considered a party in the crime.

Bertie, a beautiful feisty Jamaican of nineteen, who I later discovered was in prison for killing her four-month-old child, sat next to Dolly that first night, laughing as she grabbed at pens and paper as though they were manna in a starving wilderness. She shrugged off the shunning from some who called her "baby killer." She shrugged her shoulders at me when she learned that she was in English class ("It's either you or ESL"). Bertie saun-tered, had a Modigliani neck, brown arms shimmering in a sleeveless orange shirt, and dressed more for posh downtown Boston than for Framingham. She eventually wrote about growing up in rural Jamaica, where she loved her pet goat, took her to school for show-and-tell, and was not prepared for the night her mother decided to serve the goat to company for dinner. Out behind the house, Bertie had found her beloved goat's head—in a pot.

After I heard of what Bertie experienced as her mother's betrayal, I thought long and hard about what kind of life she must have had. In fact, each woman was a book to me, teaching me as much as I was teaching them. Although Bertie's despair didn't justify her killing her child, it cer-tainly clarified that everyone has a story, a complicated history. Bertie strug-gled with herself in class journal writing, where for the first time she began to write about her crime.

These were the days before uniforms, when women had boom boxes and earrings, when they could dry their hair with a blow-dryer, when letters to home were not unsealed, and when private companies hadn't taken over medical care and phone service. These were the days when Mamie, a black woman, fell and was ignored for so long that she had to be shipped out before they finally diagnosed her with cancer, when Rose came to class to get away from her HIV diagnosis that kept her an outsider in the prison. Kit, the class clown, an Irish American considered scraggly—more a homeless woman than an inmate—had her teeth taken away because they "could be used as a weapon." Like many women behind bars, she had her kids sent to the Department of Social Services because there was no father, no sister or mother to help out. Kit said she came to class to "learn another way of living than the streets."

The women's lives seemed as large as Shakespeare's characters. I often wondered how to proceed. I saw that they had toughed it out in a society that favors others by gender, class, or race. "They seemed Desdemonas suffering because of jealous men, Lady Macbeths craving the power of their spouses, Portias disguised as men in order to get ahead, and Shylocks who, being betrayed, take the law into their own hands" (Trounstine, 2001, p. 2). Although I began as I began everywhere—with books, pen, and paper—one day during the end of the first year as a college prison teacher I lucked upon teaching Shakespeare.

On the Road to the First Production

Dolly reminded me in the middle of that first year that men behind bars were offered more than women: more college classes, job opportunities, and exercise; a better law library; less harassment from officers. The crowning blow for her was when *The Man of La Mancha,* performed by male prisoners, toured the year before. Why, she asked, could the women not even get a chance to perform in a play, never mind tour other prisons? It was Dolly's suggestion that catapulted me, reminding me that empowerment comes from the collaborative bond between student and teacher, touching feminist and activist chords. I had to find a way to get a play program at Framingham.

That fall, after attending a National Endowment for the Humanities seminar in England and getting a grant to do a play at the prison, I entered Framingham with scripts in hand: *The Merchant of Venice.* I planned to direct two productions, one at the high school and one at the prison. I planned to have the two groups correspond and learn from each other; this was somewhat idealistic, but I naïvely imagined a "cross-cultural experiment." I'd seen *Merchant* in England that summer. I felt the themes of mercy and justice would intrigue the women and encourage them to question how Portia manages to succeed in her trial. I thought they'd be sympathetic with Shylock, who, once betrayed by his daughter, feels he must keep face and have revenge, his pound of flesh. They would understand as much as anyone that

New Directions for Adult and Continuing Education • DOI: 10.1002/ace

what the court ultimately does in the name of justice—take away Shylock's religion—might not be truly just. But it was not simply the themes that mattered to the women. They were happy to be able to put on a play—something they saw as fun, distracting, and hopeful—and at first it didn't really matter that they had no commerce with the Bard. I felt (and still do) that to give students what they think most difficult—Shakespeare, in this case—and see them succeed allows them to imagine endless possibilities.

The women loved it when I first told them the tale, warming quickly to the idea that a trial might be appealing behind bars. Bertie was the first to balk, insisting that there was no way we were going to say "thou" and "hast" onstage. The others wanted to find a way to make sure they wouldn't look like fools in front of their peers. It didn't matter that I knew they would eventually respond to Shakespeare's amazing story, that the text would lead them. The language was a barrier. Their resistance and fear forced me to find a way to unwrap the script.

Thus one of my major teaching techniques came from them. As we sat around in a circle, it seemed necessary for us to read aloud. I suggested they paraphrase each line, putting Shakespeare's words into their own. As they struggled to find metaphors that made sense ("Wouldst thou have a serpent sting thee twice" became "What? You wanna have a pit bull attack you twice?")—they started to translate the language. They laughed at Shakespeare's jokes and nudged each other at some of the characters' actions they found disturbing. This paraphrasing gave them a chance to feel heard within the text; it engaged their emotions and allowed the text to resonate with their experiences. But it was Shakespeare's ideas, characters, humor, and pathos that had the power to engage. The text was the teacher.

How Education Behind Bars Becomes Political

There is no way that learning in prison does not occur for the teacher as much as for the student. After all, I knew nothing about what their lives were like inside and found myself constantly having to adjust my thinking. Who could imagine that a woman going for a breast exam would get leg-chained in a van? Who could know that a guard would put his hand on a prisoner, suggesting they meet alone at "count" or that another would bet me on a particular prisoner's demise? Working in an environment that is outside the control of both teacher and student actually fosters closeness between the two, exactly what the prison fears (for the teacher—"You can't go in today, there's been a riot"; for the student—"You have to stay in your unit because so-and-so tried to hang herself"). Collaboration is what many in power fear because it empowers the prisoner. For my part, it increased my dedication and my activism. As I began to understand that women often received harsher sentences than men, we read Doris Lessing's *A Woman on a Roof* (1991) and Shakespeare's *The Taming of the Shrew*. When the women talked about being ignored by guards when they were ill, kept in holding tanks at hospitals, and waist-chained while waiting for exams, we read Zora Neale Hurston's *Sweat* (1997). While they complained about the relationships they had with abusive men, we considered Henrik Ibsen's *The Doll's House* (2005). John Howard Griffin's *Black Like Me* (1961) and *Nobody Mean More to Me Than You and the Future Life of Willy Jordan* by June Jordan (1988) allowed us to touch on the issue of race. After every class behind bars, my high schoolers wanted to hear about the prisoners. They wanted to study *Merchant* because the inmates were studying it, and they formed a group, the Prison Issues Project, to write, read, and learn about women behind bars.

I began to see the inherently political nature of education: to free one's mind. Although Freire (1990) wants us to think in terms of teacher-student and student-teacher—that is, a teacher who learns and a learner who teaches—as the basic roles of classroom participation, I discovered that learning often becomes collaborative because both student and teacher are creating in an environment that does not want creativity. In a sense, communal activism gets fostered through the oppressive prison environment.

None of this was discussed openly in my prison classroom, but we all understood that rebellious moments were intrinsic behind bars. We resisted those who tried to curb our thinking, and we resisted pointless rules. The women shared clothing, had "illegal" sexual contact, bartered for cigarettes. I found myself gleeful at getting away with things in an environment that often said no without any logical reason, that infantilized women and demeaned them. They smoked secretly or asked me to mail letters for them (buying stamps took part of the little money they had), and I got enormous joy out of hiding my thin gold necklace beneath my turtleneck when I was searched. I fostered my high schoolers' sending letters to the inmates, and although I kept a note from each prisoner with permission to give out names, I knew the prison would not have allowed this contact. When they tried on Shakespearean costumes one evening and went parading up and down the halls to show their friends (without permission), they caused such a commotion that the officers "wrote me up." Luckily, the women were not penalized. If the administration had cared as much about the content of my plays as they did about "appropriate behavior," I cannot imagine I would have lasted ten years.

Education behind bars cannot help but be defiant because freeing the mind is in direct opposition to closing it up. The question I raised for myself applied to the women as well; theater could lead them to think through their actions and step inside someone else's shoes, providing a real change in perspective. Theater allowed them, as Rose said, "to be someone else, if only for a one night." They reimagined themselves onstage.

I saw the potential of theater to affect the internal life, but I also saw that theater could be enormously political. When we decided to have Portia come undisguised as a woman in the courtroom—altering Shakespeare's original text—not only were we setting up a female in a male world, urging the audience to see how ably she handles it, but we empowered them and thus the audience. Putting Shakespeare's words into their own vernacular allowed everyone to take charge and feel part of the creation.

Freire (1990) talks about transformation as a direct contradiction to filling people with facts ("the banking concept of education"), and like Freire I was discovering that education could foster opportunities for reflection and change. "The solution is not to 'integrate' them [students] into the structure of oppression, but to transform that structure so that they [students] can become 'beings for themselves'" (p. 61). This is inherently political because it does not always conform to institutional mores. Thus the students learned to do a play, tackle Shakespeare, and think for themselves. I learned to speak out and stand up for them.

The Production

It took six months for us to study, rehearse, and eventually perform the play. Most of the work was done in the classroom, and many production decisions were collaborative. They watched with interest two film versions of *The Merchant of Venice* and decided that they liked the Sir Lawrence Olivier version better, wanting our ending to suggest Shylock's taking his own life because of the cruelty of the court. They found someone to paint a set for us; they made props (a knife, a scale) when we needed them, as well as posters to advertise the production. Rhonda, an inmate who'd gone to college and after losing her father dropped out and turned to drugs, had the most experience with Shakespeare. She jumped in and typed up our script. Rhonda had found her way back to the classroom because she said it was close to her roots. All the women wanted her to be Portia. "You know I was a pre-law student before prison," she wrote me years later, after release, a child, two jobs, and a college degree.

The production itself was held in the gym, where we set up chairs for more than two hundred other inmates. It was for the performers a night outside prison, where they experienced themselves whole again and not only pulled off Shakespeare but got the audience involved in the themes of the play. They were heralded by two hundred inmates, several of whom talked back during the production ("You can't take away a man's religion"; "There's nothin' wrong with bein' a Jew if that's what you are"). The audience cheered; several wept. Later, Dolly said she felt like a star. They all talked about how much more confidence they had, and they all wanted to do more plays. Bertie couldn't get over how much her accent had improved. Kit, the class clown, wanted her kids to have a tape of the performance, to show that she'd really been a part of something to be proud of. Experience had led to the deepest kind of learning.

New Directions for Adult and Continuing Education • DOI: 10.1002/ace

My high schoolers saw a tape of the play and continued to write their pen pals long after the production. Dolly wrote a letter of recommendation to help one student get into Wellesley, and Rhonda saw the young man she wrote go to Brown. The Prison Issues Project existed for several years, even after I began teaching at the community college, because as one student said, "My exposure to prison changed me." I directed seven more plays, all based on classic texts, ranging from a rap version of *The Taming of the Shrew* to an adaptation of *The Scarlet Letter,* a play set in three centuries with the "A" standing not only for adultery but also for "abuse" and "AIDS."

Theater is transformative because it opens the mind. When minds open behind bars, you are working against the nature of prison: confinement of mind as well as confinement of body.

Changing Lives Through Literature

Five years into my work behind bars, I heard about a little-known alternative sentencing program that announced it could "change lives." By now, I knew that many returned to prison, in part because people getting out often are without jobs and have unsettled relationships, questionable housing, and minimal support from a community. I knew how frustrating it was for the inmates to go back to their cramped cells, to continue in the same conditions, in spite of the amazing work they did onstage. They were always confronted with literal restrictions even as they sought to be free in the classroom. Though I saw change, I also saw the limitations of the grueling day-to-day of incarceration.

Changing Lives Through Literature (CLTL) was a program for offenders outside prison that had begun in the fall of 1991. Judge Robert Kane, then a district court judge, and Robert Waxler, a professor at the University of Massachusetts, Dartmouth, wondered if a probation program might have better results than prison in stimulating life change. Corrections likes to talk about change only in terms of recidivism—how much, how often, and in what ways people return to crime. But Kane and Waxler were interested in the thinking behind the choices offenders made. They wondered what might affect those choices. Kane's experiment began by offering eight men probation instead of prison, with an important stipulation: they had to complete a Modern American Literature seminar run by Waxler, held on the college campus. The idea was simple but profound, and one I knew in my bones: literature could be a road to insight, and insight could pave the way to change.

For the first program, Wayne St. Pierre, a New Bedford District Court probation officer (PO), checked out the men's basic reading ability by having them read and discuss a short article. The first seminar was held for twelve weeks with men who had not graduated from high school and who had among them 148 convictions for crimes such as armed robbery and theft. The team wanted the program to be seen as "serious," having no chance of being considered "soft on crime." Kane, Waxler, and St. Pierre insisted on a "democratic" classroom where all ideas were valid.

This idea—a group consisting of student-offenders, the judge who sentenced them to the program, and one or more probation officers who handled their cases—brought me on board. Literature discussion groups with offenders on the same playing field as judges and POs seemed unheard of in our criminal justice system. The belief that everyone's opinion about the story *mattered* and no one had the final say democratized the conversation.

By discussing books and the characters who inhabit them, the first group of men began to investigate and explore new aspects of themselves, as well as increase their ability to communicate ideas and feelings to each other and to the judge, professor, and probation officers—all symbols of authority who they thought would never listen. They were heard, and they discovered that their opinions held weight. Participants reported that each person's experience led him to his own way of seeing the same text. Instead of seeing their world from only one angle, they began opening up to new points of view, gained confidence, became more articulate, and started realizing they had more choices in life. Equally profound were the experiences of the judge, POs, and professor, who also reported having been changed by the class.

Jack Mezirow (1991) talks about this kind of learning as the giving up of beliefs, attitudes, and emotional reactions and says it occurs when people engage in critical reflection on their experience, which leads to a perspective transformation. Mezirow (1978) says transformative learning involves the "conscious recognition of the difference between [his] old viewpoint and the new one" that leads the learner to see that there is more value in the new perspective (p. 105).

This seemed similar to what I had experienced behind bars. With Dolly's words in my mind—that men always were always offered the best programs—and the certainty that women might benefit from CLTL, I met with Kane and Waxler about beginning an all-female program. I knew that the issues for women offenders in a reading group might be different from those for men. Because forces in our society compel females to be nurturers and encourage the "American dream"—two and a half children, a spouse, and a happy home in a white-picket-fence neighborhood—they blame themselves for scars on the family, for poverty, and most of all for crippling the lives of their children. They have difficulty not depending on men and often choose people who mistreat them, proving to themselves that they aren't worth much. Women of color face even more pressures than white women as they struggle with a higher incarceration rate for their family members and more issues of poverty and societal racism. Certainly women of all ethnicities who came into my prison classes had a lack of confidence about their ability to succeed in the world. The women in CLTL would be more afraid to fail than their male counterparts. This I believed.

New Directions for Adult and Continuing Education • DOI: 10.1002/ace

In 1992, we initiated our first women's program. Quickly, we realized we needed to join two courts together to have enough women to enable powerful discussion, and so the Lynn-Lowell program began. Soon after, men's and women's programs spread throughout the state and throughout the country to include Arizona, California, Connecticut, Indiana, Kansas, Maine, New York, Rhode Island, Texas, and the UK. Programs are held in colleges, libraries, halfway houses, and prisons. Some are singled-gendered; some are mixed, and in the great tradition of experiment some add writing. But the basic concept—literature, discussion, and equal playing field—remains at our program's core and fosters the democratic classroom. In 2004, we created a Website to continue developing the program across the country (http://cltl.umassd.edu); more than forty-three hundred people have graduated from the program in the past fifteen years.

The format of the class is simple. Facilitators, often professors, choose material for everyone to read. We usually sit around a table, fostering the idea of discussion with all and for all. We are in essence a reading group but tend to stick to the text and ideas brought up by the text; this is not therapy but a way to get the text to be the teacher. I usually ask my students how they feel about reading at the first class, but their pasts come up only as they talk about books. Some facilitators use small group discussion; others keep the two-hour class in one large group. As we talk about the book, its characters and themes, we consider large questions of ethics and morality, why characters make the choices they do, and what effects each behavior choice has. Although there will be moments when participants make profound connection to their own lives, the point is to discuss the characters and talk about ideas. We want them to see themselves through others; the personal is revealed through the universal. Most important, because we are not agenda-driven, the classroom stays a safe place where no one is right and likewise no experience is wrong.

In one class where we were reading Toni Morrison's *The Bluest Eye,* this became quite clear to me. We were talking about Cholly, the father of Pecola, a young black girl. Pecola believes that if she gets blue eyes, she will have access to a Shirley Temple world and all her pain and suffering will disappear. In a way, she does get these blue eyes at the end of the book, after her father has sexually molested her and she has been teased mercilessly in school, gone to a town shaman, and lost her sanity. Morrison makes sure we know that such "gifts" do not ensure happiness.

In our discussion, one of the women in our racially mixed group turned to the part of the novel she wanted to discuss. The probationer asked us to look at a particularly painful passage, where Cholly rapes Pecola. She said, "Do you think Cholly really believes that is love?" At first there was stunned silence in the room as we thought about her question. The men—our dedicated Judge Joseph Dever (cofounder with me of the Women's Program) and one of the POs—said "No!" and tended to want to push the question aside because it was so uncomfortable for them. But the women wanted to explore the question, to understand what was in Cholly's mind. They could not stop talking about how and why Cholly might think that he was truly loving his daughter with his actions. They pondered his background, his losses, his social understandings as well as Pecola's. It was clear that several of them were alive to their own abuse experiences at the same time, and that without talking about themselves they were processing deeply on two levels, the level of the text and the level of self. Someone said that she understood that there was hope for all of us because there is hope for Claudia, the young narrator who tells the story.

This seeming duality—discussion of the literature while recognizing one's own experiences—promotes thought and potential change. It is in part why I have always found literature such a powerful tool. Reading alone allows reflection, moral consideration, empathy, and insight. Discussion allows a kind of distancing, a gained perspective. As one female graduate, Kim, later wrote, "The judge, probation officer, and teacher . . . were all there for us. . . . It was their belief in the program and us that helped me deal with a lot of shame. They respected me until I could learn to respect myself."

Observations and Reflections

Like Annie Sullivan, I once longed to be a miracle worker. But alas, teaching is not about creating miracles, and teaching those in conflict with the law is even less so. I've had to learn how to get out of the way of learning, how to be a facilitator, a good Joker. When I consider how the students I teach change, I see that books have been a vehicle and that the word *offender* has little to do with their potential.

Institutions resist change, but in spite of that people have power. The question I first posed to myself is always being answered anew, each time I meet a new class and choose new books, in essence how to provide experiences that hopefully will be the way to insight and thus to better lives. I am not naïve enough to believe that art is the only thing we need, but I do believe that ideas can soar behind bars and books can reach inside us, as gently as a slight breeze or as fiercely as a caged bird.

References

Boal, A. *Theatre of the Oppressed*. London: Pluto Press, 1979.
Freire, P. *Pedagogy of the Oppressed*. New York: Continuum Press, 1990.
Freire, P. *Pedagogy of Hope: Reliving the Pedagogy of the Oppressed*. New York: Continuum, 1994.
Griffin, J. H. *Black Like Me*. Boston: Houghton Mifflin, 1961.
Grotowski, J. *Towards a Poor Theatre*. New York: Simon and Schuster, 1970.
Hurston, Z. N. *Sweat*. New Brunswick, N.J.: Rutgers University Press, 1997.

Ibsen, H. *The Doll's House*. Clayton, Del.: Prestwick House, Literary Touchstone Press, 2005.

Jordan, J. "Nobody Mean More to Me Than You and the Future Life of Willy Jordan." *Harvard Educational Review,* 1988, *58*(3), 363–374.

Kaltenhauser, S. "The Prison Playwright." *Gadfly,* Sept.-Oct. 1999. Retrieved July 14, 2007, from http://www.gadflyonline.com/archive/SepOct99/archive-playwright.html.

Lessing, D. "A Woman on a Roof." In S. Barnet (ed.), *The Harper Anthology of Fiction.* White Plains, N.Y.: Longman, 1991.

Mezirow, J. "Perspective Transformation." *Adult Education,* 1978, *28*(2), 100–110.

Mezirow, J. *Transformative Dimensions of Adult Learning.* San Francisco: Jossey-Bass, 1991.

Morrison, T. *The Bluest Eye.* New York: Plume, 2000.

Neill, A. "Criticism, Ethics and the Problem of Rehabilitation." *Law, Culture, and the Humanities,* 2006, *2*(2), 284–300.

Rogers, C. *Freedom to Learn: A View of What Education Might Become.* (Center for the Studies of the Person.) New York: Merrill, 1969.

Trounstine, J. *Shakespeare Behind Bars: The Power of Drama in a Women's Prison.* New York: St. Martin's Press, 2001.

JEAN TROUNSTINE *is an author, activist, and professor of humanities at Middlesex Community College in Massachusetts who has won many awards for her work.*

7

This chapter describes the methodology of the Theater of the Oppressed as developed by Augusto Boal along with examples of its application.

Democratic Process and the Theater of the Oppressed

Marie-Claire Picher

For more than forty years, the Theater of the Oppressed (TO), founded by the Brazilian cultural revolutionary and popular educator Augusto Boal, has been serving oppressed communities the world over as a powerful tool for building community and organizing for direct democracy (Picher, 2006). TO embodies the concept of theater as political act—both a transfer of cultural power to the oppressed and a *rehearsal for revolution* (Boal, 1985). "All the truly revolutionary theatrical groups," says Boal (1985), "should transfer to the people the means of production in the theater so that the people themselves may utilize them" (p. 122).

Aesthetic Education for Liberation

Within the framework of the poetics of TO, the aesthetic or artistic function of theater is dialectically connected to its pedagogical function (Boal, 2006). TO highlights theater not as spectacle but rather as a learning process that fosters critical thinking. Specifically, TO is understood as a practice consistent with Paulo Freire's approach to liberatory education—namely, aesthetic education that promotes a transformative model of learning based on dialogue. In TO, this dialogue is brought about through creation of a playful environment in which people express, analyze, and collectively change images of their reality according to their desires (Boal, 1998). Play structures are accordingly designed to activate a problem-posing learning process where participants examine and analyze their reality. First

NEW DIRECTIONS FOR ADULT AND CONTINUING EDUCATION, no. 116, Winter 2007 © 2007 Wiley Periodicals, Inc.
Published online in Wiley InterScience (www.interscience.wiley.com) • DOI: 10.1002/ace.278

they create images based on their own direct experiences; then they analyze the power relations and root causes of the oppression expressed within those images; and finally they act to transform the situation according to their vision of possible alternatives. TO thus involves itself in the struggle to change consciousness; it engages the oppressed in a dialectical process of understanding the ideology of oppression and of creating new ideologies based on their desires.

Aesthetic education transcends art for art's sake, for it contributes to creating a participatory culture that promotes the right of everyone to fully participate in the organization, maintenance, and transformation of daily life. In addition, it helps develop the necessary capacities for that participation (Boal, 2006). TO is an intentional walk toward what in Latin American popular movements is known as *horizontalidad*, that is, equality in decision making, as well as development of the consciousness and capacities needed to practice equality (Sitrin, 2006).

In TO, theory and practice form an integrated system; they constitute a *praxis* that is rooted in the struggle to change consciousness, and this struggle emerges as the art of organizing for direct democracy by using direct democracy. Let us examine this system more closely.

The Theory

The theory of TO rests on six basic tenets. First, we as human beings are by definition creators; we are inherently artists and actors who organize and transform our surroundings (Boal, 2006). The second tenet is an extension of the first: we are also inherently "theater," in terms of social consciousness and social interaction. On the one hand, as conscious beings we play the roles of actor *and* spectator, or observer, of ourselves; on the other, we are engaged in developing our innate capacity for dialogue with ourselves and with others. We thus engage in a dialectic of action and reflection, acting on and transforming our environment and simultaneously transforming ourselves, because we are part of that environment. Boal refers to this dimension of our humanity as "essential theater" (Boal, 2002).

The third tenet introduces an egalitarian ethos: it is the responsibility of society to help all people develop their innate capacity for creativity, consciousness, and dialogue. The use of direct participatory democracy is the most effective means to achieve this (Boal, 2006). The fourth is concerned with the ethical poverty of capitalist society. The global market economy, which transforms natural resources and landbases into private property to generate monetary profit, destroys people and the environment. Characterized by the concentration of political, social, and economic power, as well as by hierarchical structure, which are all fundamentally antithetical to direct democracy, the market economy is exceedingly dehumanizing, inhibiting the development of full human potential (Boal, 1998).

New Directions for Adult and Continuing Education • DOI: 10.1002/ace

The fifth tenet considers the hegemony of bourgeois ideology as a system of political positions, educational theories, attitudes, beliefs, and feelings. It takes into account the flexibility of this ideology to perpetuate itself and capitalism. The dominant ideology validates exploitation and domination, for example, by making them appear natural and necessary (Boal, 2006). More important, we all "carry" capitalism within ourselves; that is, we ideologically internalize it. The sixth and final tenet proposes that transforming images of reality according to our desires and dreams is in itself a transformative act.

Confronted by the intellectual domination of art and education by the ruling elites, TO takes a militant stand: it challenges bourgeois theory and cultural practices by engaging in a battle around culture. Boal conceives of and practices TO as a *martial art*, whose primary function is to serve simultaneously as a weapon of resistance against oppression and a tool for creating a transformative culture.

The guiding ethical imperative expressed by Boal in his *The Aesthetics of the Oppressed* consists of (1) rejection of the ideology of political "neutrality" that dominates education and the arts; (2) affirmation of the inherent political function of art; and (3) action, the creation of an oppositional and emancipatory model of theater based on democratic principles—theater of, by, and for the oppressed who are fighting back and creating a new society. In practice, this model of aesthetic education consists of transferring to oppressed communities knowledge about the means of production in theater: "how to" as well as "what" and "why," "for whom" and "for what purpose" (Boal, 2006, pp. 44–51). Thus the collective lack of democratic experience is overcome by breaking with the behavior of nonparticipation.

As the practice of theater is demystified and made accessible, it becomes possible for ordinary people to free themselves from the *ideology of expertise*. They rediscover and validate their own capacity for becoming actors in their own lives. Within the TO model, aesthetic education gives people the opportunity to engage, on their own terms, in a learning process where they use all available resources, including human ones, to transform their own existence as well as empower their communities.

The Practice

TO's practice can be described in terms of method and technique.

The Method. The Paulo Freire methodology frames TO's practice of aesthetic education. Its basic problem-posing steps are to see (*and* hear *and* feel), to analyze, and to act. Each step in turn embodies three propositions about the nature of the real world and is diametrically opposed to the dominant ideology of fragmentation: (1) in the real world, each person is an indivisible whole whose sensations, movements, ideas, emotions, and beliefs do not merely interact with one another but are *interwoven* with one another; (2) all ideas and mental images reveal themselves physically, that is, the psychic and physical realms are connected and overlap; (3) all five senses are linked (Boal, 2002).

Based on such humanist principles, the TO method sets in motion concepts, processes, and play structures that support the dynamics of egalitarian participation and transformation needed for people to learn theatrical production. For example, theater is emphasized as both a fundamental human activity (essential theater) and as the art of framing, examining, and playing with what we do naturally every day. The language of theater is correspondingly emphasized as something accessible to everyone. Moreover, all aesthetic activities are participatory, interactive, and improvised by participants from their direct experience of daily life. Core activities include a repertory of *exercises* (physical, muscular monologues), *games* (physical dialogues with or without words), and *techniques* (more complex structures based on a theme, or problem to be analyzed and transformed). Finally, the totality of activities make up what Boal (2006) calls a "subjunctive" theater, that is, a theater designed to question values and structures.

The Techniques. The main TO techniques are invisible theater, image theater, forum theater, and legislative theater (Boal, 2002).

Invisible theater is a skit performed in open public spaces as a real-life situation, whose goal is to stimulate civic dialogue. Ideally, the public is not aware that a "play" is unfolding.

Image theater is a repertory of games and techniques that emphasize physical dialogues, nonverbal imagery, consensus-building and problem-solving processes, and techniques for developing awareness of both objective and internalized forms of oppression. Here, the body is used to create images that help participants explore power relations and group solutions to concrete problems.

An innovative approach to community dialogue, *forum theater* is rooted in the Brazilian social justice movements of the 1950s and 1960s. It is essentially a dialogue process that begins in workshop and continues as performance to include new people. Forum theater analyzes situations of conflict involving objective, external (as opposed to internalized) oppression, in which an appropriate action to be taken is not immediately clear. Themes for development are suggested by workshop participants, who then tell actual personal stories of unresolved conflicts stemming from political or social problems of difficult solution. Skits depicting those conflicts are improvised and presented to an audience. Each story represents the perspective of an oppressed protagonist actively engaged in implementing a strategy for resolving a conflict; the protagonist's original strategy to resolve the conflict failed, however. When the skit is over, the audience discusses the strategy that was presented, and then the scene is performed once more. But now, audience members are urged to intervene by stopping the action, coming on stage to replace actors, and enacting their own strategies for resolving the conflict.

Thus, instead of remaining passive spectators the audience becomes a group of active "spect-actors" involved in creating alternative solutions and thus controlling the dramatic action. The aim of the forum is not to find an ideal solution but to invent new ways of confronting oppression.

Legislative theater is an expansion of forum theater in the political arena of legislation (1998). It was developed by Boal during his tenure as a member of the Rio de Janeiro City Council (1993–1997). It seeks to involve people and communities directly in the process of writing laws and formulating public policy.

The Method in Action

TO's method of aesthetic education is based on a web of processes that embody dialectical principles of participation and transformation. Like multiple self-reflecting mirrors, these processes are integrated into the structure of every activity (Boal, 2002). The core processes are *dialogue* and the *primacy of process over product*. From these two flow others, including (1) the logic of moving from the simple to the more complex; (2) improvisation; (3) "dynamization," or animation of static images through movement, sound, and words in relationship to other images, in view of mobilizing desires; (4) scrutinizing direct experience, and seeking to reveal contradictions within images and discussions of real life; (5) the dialectical relationship between the individual and the collective; (6) communication based on seeing and hearing others, reciprocity and openness to change; (7) sympathy, or "reciprocal empathy" (Boal, 1995); (8) horizontal and cooperative leadership models; (9) dialectical integration of actors and spectators into spect-actors; and (10) collective strategizing to confront and eradicate oppression.

Let us examine how these processes function in a few typical activities.

Game: Colombian Hypnosis. Description: the group breaks down into pairs; one person is a leader and the other a follower. The follower's eyes are fixated on the palm of the leader's hand (leaders are responsible for the safety of their partners). There are three steps: (1) with one hand, leaders silently guide their partners in movement very slowly through the space. (2) After a few minutes, leader and follower exchange roles. (3) Finally, both hypnotize each other simultaneously. After the game, partners discuss with one another what they experienced and observed, and what skills were activated. Variations on this exercise include groups of three, and the whole group simultaneously leading and following (Boal, 2002).

The dynamics of collaboration and consensus are built into the structure of this group integration game. As participants help their partners focus on body language and expand their range of movement, they coordinate patterns, practice cooperation, and build trust. Emphasis can be placed on developing the capacity to practice horizontal forms of leadership, based on open, two-way dialogue.

New Directions for Adult and Continuing Education • DOI: 10.1002/ace

Image Theater Game. The most basic is Complete the Image. Description: (1) two actors silently improvise a static image by shaking hands; the group then projects meanings onto the image by free association. (2) Each actor in turn steps out of the image and then returns with a new body position. (3) One by one, observers replace one character and then the other, each time inventing a new way to complete the existing image by positioning their own bodies differently. (4) The group repeats the process, without projecting meanings, in groupings of two, three, or more (Boal, 2002).

In this game, an "embodied" metaphor of the Freirian problem-posing steps, participants (1) explore the language of images, that is, images as surfaces that reflect multiple meanings projected onto them; (2) reflect on the relation among perception, perspective, and meaning; (3) shift perspectives and begin to modify patterns of perception; and (4) practice transforming situations by means of body juxtaposition and repositioning.

The whole method of Theatre of the Oppressed, and particularly of the image theater series, is based on the multiple mirror of the gaze of others—a number of people looking at the same image, and offering their feelings and what is evoked for them. This multiple reflection reveals to the person who made the image its hidden aspects (Boal, 2002).

Image Theater Technique. Let us pick the Image of Transition from the Real to the Ideal. Description: (1) participants "sculpt" an image of a real problem common to all, using as many characters as needed; the final form of the image is chosen by consensus. (2) Observers describe the formal qualities of the image and then project onto it subjective meanings. (3) Observers resculpt the same characters into an image of the ideal situation—a possible desired "real" that has not yet materialized; the final form of the image is also decided by consensus. (4) One by one, observers modify the initial image by creating images of possible transitions from the real to the ideal. (5) Characters create their own version of possible transitions from the real to the ideal, according to their desires, by dynamizing the image. (6) Actors and observers compare experiences and observations (Boal, 2002).

This activity consists of exploring the ideology of oppression by creating group images of oppression and desires. Practicing consensus, participants create and develop characters flowing out of still body positions that emerge from their experience, and finally through movement transform an oppressive situation into a desired reality. This use of nonverbal body imagery helps a group clarify its understanding of a problem by visualizing it, and collectively explore options for resolving it; it also offers the group a powerful medium for examining stereotypes and clarifying its own vision. Other techniques similar to this one, such as "Cop in the Head" (Boal, 1995), analyze internalized oppression through more complex character development and a focus on oppressors' tactics. As participants analyze the mechanisms of oppression that operate in various situations, they experience how the power of oppression extends from one space to another, and how common experiences go beyond the particularities of individual stories.

Forum Theater. Forum theater is designed to maximize participation of the audience in a performance by shifting the central focus of the dramatic event from the stage to the audience. This shift occurs through the spect-actor principle. The concept refers both to a social relation and to a protagonistic function; rather than being installed into fixed roles, as in conventional theater, the spectators and actors have dual functions, mobile and reciprocal, and the theatrical action becomes one that all participants— actors and audience—can exercise. The spect-actor function is fundamental to all TO activities; in forum theater it creates a new performance mode. First, actors recognize the audience as equal performance partners from the very start; before the dramatic action starts, they play and dialogue with the audience through group integration exercises and games. Thus expansion of the aesthetic space into the audience area begins. Second, the first time an audience member interrupts the dramatic action, the focus of the performance shifts from the stage to the newly established aesthetic space comprising both stage *and* audience area; what occurs in this space is shared dramaturgy (Boal, 2002). Third, by taking on the role of protagonists of the dramatic action, audience members prepare to be protagonists of their own lives in the much broader social sphere.

In forum theater, the spect-actor role play is a vehicle for analyzing power and stimulating public debate. Participants explore the complexity of the individual-group relation at a variety of levels. They are invited to map out (1) the dynamics of power within and between groups; (2) the experience and the fear of powerlessness within the individual; and (3) rigid patterns of perception that generate miscommunication and conflict, as well as ways of transforming them. Forum theater is useful as a means of helping participants prepare for effective social action intended to transform the objective social and political realities of their community. Such actions include public forums, strikes, demonstrations, and other types of direct action.

A Community Organizing Tool

In TO, democracy is not only a vision but also a practice rooted in the daily life of oppressed people. The cultural struggle in which TO is engaged in more than seventy countries can best be understood as a liberatory project: that of actualizing processes of direct democracy. This practice, however, takes different forms according to the social and political context of the country. In Brazil, for example, Boal's Center (CTO-RIO; ctorio@ctorio.org.br.) works on human rights issues with many groups in poor communities.

Long-term projects, some of which have brought about municipal legislation, have been created with slum dwellers, street children, teachers, housemaids, and mental health self-advocates. Another project, located in seven Brazilian states, has boosted the prison reform movement through a program involving both prison personnel and prisoners. The landless peasant movement (MST) now includes TO as a basic component of its organizer training.

In the Calcutta region of India, the work of the collective Jana Sanskriti has given rise to a large TO-based political movement of peasants and agricultural workers—more than twelve hundred groups—who organize around issues of hunger, unemployment, and unionizing. In Paris, an early TO center, groups presently work within immigrant communities on issues of immigrants' rights and homelessness. To consult the TO International Yellow Pages, go to www.theatreoftheoppressed.org.

The New York-based Theater of the Oppressed Laboratory (TOPLAB), which has maintained a close working relationship with Boal and CTO-Rio since 1990, has offered training to a spectrum of activists and organizers confronting numerous social issues and issues of oppression, such as housing, health care, substance abuse, HIV-AIDS, violence, racism, sexism, and discrimination based on gender orientation and ethnicity. This work has included leadership development projects in public schools such as the Renaissance School in Queens, as well as partnerships with community organizations such as Make the Road by Walking, Cabrini Immigrant Services/Justice for Immigrants Campaign at Saint Teresa's, Jews for Racial and Economic Justice, Mothers on the Move, and Quilombo Summer.

Two Recent TOPLAB Community-Based Projects

The first is Make the Road by Walking (MRBW). In January 2006, TOPLAB began a working partnership with MRBW, a Brooklyn community organization that promotes economic justice and direct democracy. Members of MRBW are predominantly low-income Latino and African American residents of the Bushwick section and nearby communities. The project involved members of BASTA, MRBW's environmental and housing justice subcommittee, which primarily fights for tenant rights and increasing green space for marginalized communities in New York City.

The first phase of this partnership was a six-month facilitator training program in image and forum theater, in which MRBW was one of four participating groups. The program was designed as an "internship with practicum" whose purpose was to help participating groups create a ten-minute problem-posing forum theater skit. It consisted of a series of monthly workshops for interns—the groups' representatives—held at the Brecht Forum in Manhattan, practice sessions with the community group and intracommunity performances held directly in the interns' respective communities, and an intercommunity theater festival.

To participate in the program, BASTA members formed the Make the Road Theater Collective. Their objective was to incorporate forum theater into their community mobilizing efforts. Members hoped to develop abilities they felt were needed to make their educational outreach and organizing campaigns more inclusive and effective: nonhierarchical leadership dynamics, self-confidence, self-activity and creativity, open dialogue, and problem-solving skills for planning actions. They also wanted to develop new perspectives on how to create fresh and playful approaches to their meetings and actions.

During the six-month period, BASTA integrated TO practices into its organizational structure, including movement, body sculpting, improvisation, creation of problem-posing plays in view of audience participation and collective strategizing, consensus, and nonauthoritarian leadership.

By strengthening their artistic capacity, BASTA members also developed fresh approaches to community action and organizational dynamics. Integration of theater into meetings and actions has made them more participatory and enjoyable and as a result has kept community members involved and attracted new members. Communication among organizers and members has also improved.

The TOPLAB partnership with MRBW is now in its second phase. A new street theater and forum theater project, coordinated by BASTA and involving other citywide environmental justice groups, has recently been formed and is developing its own working model.

The second project is the Cabrini Immigrant Services/Justice for Immigrants (JFI) Campaign at Saint Teresa's. In February 2007, TOPLAB began a partnership with the JFI Campaign at Saint Teresa's Church on New York's Lower East Side. The project has three components: (1) involvement in the campaign, (2) on-site TO workshops, and (3) cofacilitation with the JFI organizer. JFI campaign members have formed a theater collective in the hopes that TO will help create dialogue in the community between people interested in immigration reform and those who have remained uninvolved owing to lack of awareness of the issues.

The main objectives of the theater collective are to better understand the issues, form a support group, share experiences, use theater to communicate their concerns to their community, explore strategies of persuasion, and plan a short-term action. Members have also committed to working together in a spirit of confidentiality, transparency, respect for others' experiences and opinions, cooperation, and love.

The first phase of the project has consisted of creating and rehearsing a forum theater skit for the parish community. At the end of a three-month rehearsal period, community members will have performed a problem-posing skit based on images created from their experiences of immigration and of the parish community. They will also have engaged in power analysis based on these images. The second phase of the project involves intra- and inter-community performances. A third phase involves training members of the theater collective as facilitators of image and forum theater.

Summary

The cultural practice and politics of TO consists of promoting not only social, economic, and political democracy but also democracy as a *way of life*—a way of understanding and creating everyday human relations based on values and attitudes that foster direct democracy. Understood within this context, TO helps groups and organizations engage in essential debate over strategy and process, confront the weaknesses within their own internal structure, and build a coalition with like-minded groups to work for social change.

Practiced within the popular education framework, TO simultaneously functions as a vehicle for organizing and as an integral component of the organizing process itself. Theater—the art of organizing human action in time and space—is by definition a privileged medium for examining the multidimensional structures of power and oppression, as well as for envisioning and creating new liberatory realities. When a theater practice that stresses the interdependency of its aesthetic, pedagogical, and political functions places itself in the service of organizing to achieve a democratic restructuring of society, it contributes a unique perspective on the art of organizing and community building and brings us another step closer to a just and compassionate society.

References

Boal, A. *Theatre of the Oppressed* (C. A. McBride and M.-O. Leal McBride, trans.). New York: Theatre Communications Group, 1985.

Boal, A. *The Rainbow of Desire: The Boal Method of Theatre and Therapy* (A. Jackson, trans.). London, UK: Routledge, 1995.

Boal, A. *Legislative Theatre: Using Performance to Make Politics* (A. Jackson, trans.). London, UK: Routledge, 1998.

Boal, A. *Games for Actors and Non-Actors* (2nd ed., A. Jackson trans.). London, UK: Routledge, 2002.

Boal, A. *The Aesthetics of the Oppressed* (A. Jackson trans.). London, UK: Routledge, 2006.

Picher, M.-C. *Fellowship,* 72(9–12). Nyack, N.Y.: Fellowship of Reconciliation, 2006.

Sitrin, M. (ed.). *Horizontalism: Voices of Popular Power in Argentina.* Oakland, Calif.: AK Press, 2006.

MARIE-CLAIRE PICHER is the artistic director and a cofounder (1990) of the New York-based Theater of the Oppressed Laboratory (TOPLAB; www.toplab.org) and assistant professor of French and Spanish in the Department of Modern Foreign Languages at the College of Mount Saint Vincent in the Bronx, New York.

8

This chapter brings together themes from the various practices presented by the educators who contributed to this volume for purposes of reflecting on the implications of the arts for the practice and theory of adult education.

Lessons from the Lessons Learned: Arts Change the World When . . .

Sandra Hayes, Lyle Yorks

". . . A genuine conversation is never the one that we wanted to conduct. Rather, it is generally more correct to say that we fall into conversation, or even that we become involved in it . . . a conversation has a spirit of its own . . . and that the language in which it is conducted bears its own truth within it—that it allows something to 'emerge' which henceforth exists" (Hans-Georg Gadamer, 1989, p. 383).

In February 2005, we were on a flight to Seattle to meet with a cooperative inquiry (CI) group that was inquiring into the role of the arts in fostering social change (Aprill and others, 2006). The inquiry question devised by the group was, "How and when does art release, create, and sustain transforming power for social change?" Although our formal role with the group was facilitating the inquiry process, given the nature of cooperative inquiry we became embedded in the conversation—one that was very stimulating. This particular inquiry was entirely consistent with the theoretical lens of whole-person knowing (Yorks and Kasl, 2002), based on the radical epistemology of Heron and Reason (1997, 2001) that guides our work with cooperative inquiry. On this flight, we were engaged in a lively conversation about the broader implications of the CI group's inquiry question when we became further stimulated by an article in that morning's *New York Times* about a program using theater with inmates in a federal prison. We had been discussing how we might continue the discourse about the use of the arts as an important ingredient in facilitating learning, especially transformative learning. The adult education work being done with the arts

NEW DIRECTIONS FOR ADULT AND CONTINUING EDUCATION, no. 116, Winter 2007 © 2007 Wiley Periodicals, Inc.
Published online in Wiley InterScience (www.interscience.wiley.com) • DOI: 10.1002/ace.279

as described in that article inspired us. Consequently, out of our conversation that morning and the ongoing conversations with the inquiry group emerged the idea of putting together a *New Directions* volume that would extend the ideas the group was generating about the arts, social justice, and learning. In doing so, we would also build on the conversation stimulated by an issue of *New Directions* seeking to demystify art and make a strong case for the arts as an integral part of adult education (Lawrence, 2005). This is important because, as Lawrence notes, many educators, especially those in formal settings, "are reluctant to encourage artistic forms of expression because they are themselves unfamiliar, and thus uncomfortable, with the affective dimensions of knowledge production" (p. 4). A closely related reason is concern for maintaining a clear distinction between education and therapy (Tisdell, Hanley, and Taylor, 2000).

We were particularly interested not only in how the arts could be used in the classroom but also in sustaining the conversation around how the arts can and do foster community and societal learning. The term *adult education* carries the connotation of a formal classroom, although we know that in practice the larger society is the context in which much adult education is practiced. We know as well that many practitioners of adult education do not define themselves as "professional adult educators." In this sense, the house of adult education has many rooms and diverse occupants. Through the writings in this *New Directions* volume, we seek to underscore this reality as a way of mining the possibilities available to all of us seeking to enrich ourselves and those we educate and learn with.

Putting together the chapters was itself an emergent conversation. We selected the contributors to this volume because they are involved in the education of adults and seek to transform some aspect of the human condition through the performing, visual, or literary arts. Even though all of the authors define themselves as practitioners who work with adults and work with the arts to foster learning, some are academics while others work in community settings and see themselves primarily as social activists. Hence the preceding chapters reflect a mixture of perspectives. As we framed our approach to this volume, our driving questions were:

- What can we learn further about the potential roles the arts can play in fostering individual and societal adult learning?
- What can we learn about the arts that has implications for adult learning theory?

Each resulting chapter has constituted a portal into how the arts can be integral to the learning process. Although some chapters are more analytical and others more expressive, they each include a story of the contributor's personal experience with the arts. Initially, we were not particularly directive with the contributors as to which aspects of their practice needed highlighting in their chapter. However, as we began learning from this project and were touched and educated by their stories, we offered guidance on which aspects of their practice might be foreground and which others might be useful background to the experience with the arts they were chronicling.

Emergent Themes from Diverse Voices

Having received the gift of diverse contributions, we looked inductively across the stories for the patterns that emerged for us as themes addressing the above questions. No doubt, in fact hopefully, readers will find other themes relevant to their practice.

Art Ushers People into Another Space—A Generative Learning Space. Much like physical and geographic structures, societal, organizational, and community structures shape the possibility for learning through blocking, constraining, or opening up interpersonal connections and relationships (Yorks, 2005). Fisher and Torbert (1995) argue that society places substantial barriers in the way of processes of learning. Learning, they argue, requires creation of liberating structures that allow educating toward self-correcting awareness. The arts seem to create this kind of liberating space by assisting people in seeing past the psychological, social, and culturally imposed boundaries of their life worlds. Sherre Wesley explicitly relates this point to the full range of the arts when she observes that art helps to move people beyond the familiar by suspending some of the rules that apply to how they engage in multiculturally diverse settings. This "learning space" destabilizes fixed ideas and existing identities. It does so by making room for greater diversity and therefore offers avenues for valuing differences. It helps people make space for connection in the world that the preexisting boundaries of social position tend to inhibit.

Kwayera Archer-Cunningham's work also illustrates a crossing of boundaries, namely those that are generational and come from a sense of isolation from one's cultural heritage. At Ifetayo Cultural Arts, the arts are the first step and foundation for generating a common set of cultural understandings and experiences by encouraging boundaries that are more interpersonally and interculturally permeable while at the same time protective of the members' sense of the community. The first step in community transformation is "establishing a safe place where adults believe they have something to contribute" (Chapter Three in this volume). The arts are not an end in themselves but an entryway for empowering people to author their own community intervention. The practice of Mbongi at Ifetayo Arts creates a constructive space in which new forms of engagement are defined. Their work echoes bell hooks's experience (1995) of how the arts can transgress every imposed boundary.

Although many of the boundaries that inhibit our perspectives and learning are normatively imposed, Jean Trounstine's work demonstrates the educative power of the arts for moving people beyond the psychological and physical barriers of incarceration. Theater enabled the women inmates to step into someone else's shoes and reimagine themselves by being on stage. The women's experience with Shakespeare, for example, not only affected their internal sense of self but afforded a medium for having them think for themselves, something counter to the institutional setting.

Art Makes Conflict Constructive for Learning. Art has the potential for making conflict rooted in diversity more constructive for learning. Mezirow (2000) describes transformative learning in terms of making our frames of reference more inclusive and permeable. What each author in this volume illustrates, both generally and in his or her own way, is the power art has for making psychological and societal boundaries more porous. This would seem to be a prerequisite for critical reflection on one's own habits of mind and point of view. Art creates an empathic connection that can encourage learning-within-relationship (Yorks and Kasl, 2002). How we see the "other" changes. As Arnie Aprill and Richard Townsell state, "The arts literally present an image of another person's consciousness that other learners can respond to in their own way." Integrating a process of communal art into LCDC's community development planning moved residents into a "shared 'state of grace'" in which they spoke and listened to each other with deepened respect and joy.

It should be noted that, through the arts, the river flows both ways in how the view of the other can change from the educator's perspective as well as from the learner's. Jean Trounstine was herself changed by her work with the inmates. Her perception of what it meant to be an inmate as well as her self-perception changed. She learned to speak out and stand up for them. This is an example of real colearning between educator and student.

Sherre Wesley describes her own experience participating in artistic events within the context of other ethnic settings and found that the arts can be the glue that binds people or encourages them to work through differences because, as she declares, it can be such a unifying force.

The arts are no panacea, however. As Sherre Wesley attests and as can be inferred from the stories of the other authors, the differences among us that are often the source of interpersonal and intergroup conflict are real and can be quite intractable. Yet through the arts, a space can be created where people listen and hear what might otherwise be inaccessible to them. Moreover, the learning needed for constructive conflict resolution to take place often requires some form of creativity to emerge. The visual, performing, and literary arts, as documented by the contributors to this volume, can be an effective vehicle to this end.

Art Helps to Examine What It Means to Learn from Experience. Learning from experience is one of the foundational concepts in adult learning theory. Less often discussed are the nature of and limitations of this experience. Our experience is, by definition, bounded by the patterns of interaction we create and by whose experiences we value. Ushering people into a new space, one characterized by difference and diversity and permitting empathic connection, offers an opportunity for gaining insight into another's experiences by stepping outside the constraints of one's own firsthand experience.

One realization for us, in working with these chapters, was how the role of youth as a means for educating adults may be overlooked. This first dawned on us when reading Valerie Kinloch's chapter. The activists and "teachers" were the youths and the learners were the adults, contrary to what is recognized to be the norm in traditional adult education discourse where adults learn from or with other adults. Valerie's experience demonstrates that honest descriptive stories of young people, embedded in local context, can challenge negative images and at the same time inform adult learning and activism.

In the organization Kwayera Archer-Cunningham founded, where the entry point is with youths from the community, youth as a vehicle for adult learning is not uncommon. Frequently, in the process of expressing themselves artistically young people find the courage to face trauma that leads to healing and learning for them, and by extension for the adults in their lives. Also, as she asserts in her chapter, youths are not just the impetus for a single learning for adults but for adults' continual learning and development. The experience of young adults as a conduit for adult learning tends to be underappreciated.

Through the Arts People Deconstruct and Reconstruct Self and Community. Because the arts have the potential for bringing into consciousness tacit, prelinguistic, preconscious knowing (Yorks and Kasl, 2006) and creating empathic connection among people with diverse and contradictory experiences, they are a powerful medium for fostering critical subjectivity and critical intersubjectivity. They offer people a medium for surfacing and reflecting critically on their own experiences and those of others around the same or similar phenomena. This parallels Armstrong's concept (2005) of how the arts can constitute two spaces of artistic potential: private space (self-understanding) and social space (understanding others through generative conversation about community within society). This is, of course, most intensely experienced in the Theater of the Oppressed (TO). Marie-Claire Picher describes variations in how TO creates an environment that empowers people to "express, analyze, and collectively change images of their reality according to their desires" (Chapter Seven in this volume, referring to comments by Boal).

Dewey (1980) observed that "so extensive and subtly pervasive are the ideas that set Art upon a remote pedestal, that many a person would be repelled rather than pleased if told that he enjoyed his casual recreations, in part at least, because of their esthetic quality" (p. 5). He goes on to note:

> We do not have to travel to the ends of the earth nor return many millennia in time to find peoples for whom everything that intensifies the sense of immediate living is an object of intense admiration. . . . Domestic utensils, furnishing of tent and house, rugs, mats, jars, pots, bows, spears, were wrought with such delighted care that today we hunt them out and give them places of honor in our art museums. Yet in their own time and place, such things were enhancements of the processes of everyday life. Instead of being elevated to a niche apart, they belonged to display of prowess, the manifestation of group and clan membership, worship of gods . . . all the rhythmic crises that punctuate the stream of living [pp. 6–7].

Valerie Kinloch's study brings into focus how seeking the art in our existing social and physical space as a medium for understanding and critiquing our heritage and the changes that are occurring "encourages people to engage in reflection on, discovery of, and action in the very spaces they inhabit and travel through" (Chapter Four in this volume). Using art in education as a process of creativity and expression, we can bring awareness to our surroundings and the implications of aesthetic impulses and history they represent.

Art Stimulates Action as a Precursor to Activism. People are used to thinking of action as directed toward an outcome, or linked as explicit behavior producing consequences in the external world. This view is to some extent the product of cursory readings of adult learning theory. Donald Schön's notions of reflection in action (1983), having a conversation with the context of the task at hand, and reflection on action, learning as a product of cycles of action and reflection, is often read this way. Kolb's experiential learning cycle implies a similar conceptualization of action positing reflective observation as a polar opposite of active experimentation, as do many other learning theories. Mezirow (1991) draws specific attention to reflection being a form of action, albeit initially an internal one. Reflection is itself an act of removing ourselves from external activity to enable more critical viewing of what is happening.

As we worked with these chapters, we came to understand "action" as consisting of a continuum of activity beginning with individual internal awareness in the body and reflection stimulated by one's environment, potentially leading to explicit action in the world, and to collective activity and activism. This is at the heart of what Kwayera Archer-Cunningham describes, using art to foster internal reflection that leads to reflective dialogue and discourse across generations, hence to activism in creating community responsive organizations.

Reflection as an action is a form of validity testing of our past learning and experiences (Mezirow, 1991). Concurrent with Heron's description of experiential knowing (1992), there is a prelingual dimension to this process where interaction with art helps what has been tacit become explicit to us. Once the tacit comes into awareness, we are then compelled to do some form of validity testing, during which we are obliged to emerge from the solitude of our own meaning making to communicate with others to arrive at new understanding of our experience. There is a process of broadening our perspective by crossing the boundaries natural to internal sense making. We have come to characterize this process of crossing boundaries as *bridging* and coming to understanding with others as *joining*. The power of the space the arts can establish is in initially bridging social divisions and holding the potential for joining through empathic connection by identification with and valuing of others.

We see this, for example, in Marie-Claire Picher's chapter where people are encouraged to reflect on their own oppression through aesthetic educational theater. By offering this artistic mode to people and thereby democratizing theater, she describes a method where people engage in the action of rediscovering and revaluing themselves as individuals capable of altering their own future. Her description of this action was instrumental in forming the concepts of bridging and joining. For participants in the Theater of the Oppressed, boundaries are crossed and understanding is created by joining with others.

Abby Scher offers another way of thinking about the action-to-activism continuum. Her description of the collaborative inquiry group's metaphorical reference to art as a "speed bump" is another example of how the arts can be a method for bringing what is tacit to the surface. She describes how their own internal assumptions and stories can be brought to light through the arts in a way that actually helps community organizers be more effective in their endeavor to relate to the communities they serve.

Art Is a Methodology for Community Development That Goes Beyond Events and Artifacts. As both Kwayera Archer-Cunningham and Marie-Claire Picher state, the writers in this volume see art as more than art for art's sake. As the previous themes attest, art is a way of generating new space for social, political, and cultural change through creating opportunities for communicating, stimulating, and tapping into experiential knowing to bridge barriers and join people together in community. The dominant methodology coming through these chapters is that inquiry through arts helps people tap into questions of importance to them and others in the community.

Art as a medium for inquiry can take many forms. Arnie Aprill and Richard Townsell used art as a way of fostering bridging and joining across generations and widening participation in the community development process. In doing so, they neutralized the power issues that often exclude people and favor what the experts believe the community needs, usually with other interests in mind. Abby Scher points to how Lily Yeh used art to initially get members of the community involved in changing their environment. What is dissimilar in the two examples is that neither Arnie Aprill nor Richard Townsell is an artist; rather, they introduced a process developed by an artist into the community's process. Lily Yeh, by contrast, is an artist and joined with the community.

Arts and the Practice of Adult Education

A basic tenet of adult learning theory has been that we are limited by our frames of reference. Additionally, a learner's capacity for learning is often constrained by the larger social structure and cultural environment (Tennant and Pogson, 1995). One's experiences are bounded and defined by those to which one can relate. As adult educators we need methods of permeating these boundaries.

Though the importance of the affective and aesthetic dimensions of the learning process has been recognized (see Imel, 1998; Greene, 1995), for the most part they have been background to the cognitive and rational dimensions of adult learning theory and practice. Emphasis has been placed on verbal discourse and dialogue, as well as the processing of experience through thoughtful (and at times critical) reflection. The arts promote alternative, and powerful, methods for bridging boundaries and enabling learners to expand their experience by accessing those of highly diverse others. The arts are also a way of bringing into consciousness, and finding expression for, experiences and insights that heretofore a learner has not had the capacity to express.

In doing so, the arts also have a way of making the "educator" a learner as well, leaving him or her mindful of the need for new perspectives on learners. As adult educators we have a tendency to ask people what they want (needs assessment). If they are not able to express it, we give them what we think they need.

Additionally, although learning has long been understood as a social process and attention has been given to team and group learning, as well as community change and social action, adult learning theory has focused on the autonomous learner. Autonomy, however, is just one part of the story. Building on the work of Boucouvalas (1988), we define the self, and by extension the learner, in terms of autonomy and homonomy. The same is true at the community level of learning. Perhaps the major challenge facing adult education in the twenty-first century is facilitating our capacity for living with one another, at the community level, in multicultural societies. The arts hold the potential for enabling understanding and valuing of other communities while simultaneously strengthening our understanding of one's own. What emerges from all of this is that the arts are a way of activating important dimensions of adult learning theory that are often relegated to the background of the learning process.

New Directions for Adult and Continuing Education • DOI: 10.1002/ace

The chapters have explored use of the arts largely outside the traditional class room. However, it is possible to extrapolate the methods for use with learners in a range of settings. We can import any number of artistic practices into formal settings, using them to bridge across cohorts or produce action-oriented learning. In summary, art situates learning in a way that makes the process of social learning relatable.

References

Aprill, A., Holliday, E., Jeffers, F., Miyamoto, N., Scher, A., Townsell, R., Yeh, L., Yorks, L. and Hayes, S. *Can The Arts Change the World? The Transformative Power of the Arts in Fostering and Sustaining Social Change: A Leadership for a Changing World Cooperative Inquiry.* New York: Research Center for Leadership in Action, Robert F. Wagner Graduate School of Public Service, New York University, 2006.

Armstrong, K. B. "Autophotography in Adult Education: Building Creative Communities for Social Justice and Democratic Education." In R. L Lawrence (ed.), *Artistic Ways of Knowing: Expanded Opportunities for Teaching and Learning.* New Directions for Adult and Continuing Education, no. 107. San Francisco: Jossey-Bass, 2005.

Boucouvalas, M. "An Analysis and Critique of the Concept of Self in Self-Directed Learning: Toward a More Robust Construct for Research and Practice." In M. Zukas (ed.), *Papers from the Transatlantic Dialogue: SCUTREA 1988.* Leeds, England: School of Continuing Education, University of Leeds, July 1988, 56–61.

Dewey, J. *Art as Experience.* New York: Perigee Books, 1980.

Fisher, D., and Torbert, W. R. *Personal and Organizational Transformations: The True Challenge of Continual Quality Improvement.* London: McGraw-Hill, 1995.

Gadamer, H.-G. *Truth and Method* (2nd ed., J. Weinsheimer and D. G. Marshall, trans.). New York: Crossroad, 1989.

Greene, M. *Releasing the Imagination: Essay on Education, the Arts, and Social Change.* San Francisco: Jossey-Bass, 1995.

Heron, J. *Feeling and Personhood: Psychology in Another Key.* Thousand Oaks, Calif.: Sage, 1992.

Heron, J., and Reason, P. "A Participatory Inquiry Paradigm." *Qualitative Inquiry,* 1997, *3,* 274–294.

Heron, J., and Reason, P. "The Practice of Co-operative Inquiry: Research 'with' Rather Than 'on' People." In P. Reason and H. Bradbury (eds.), *Handbook of Action Research: Participative Inquiry and Practice.* Thousand Oaks, Calif.: Sage, 2001.

hooks, b. *Art on My Mind.* New York: New Press, 1995.

Imel, S. "Transformative Learning in Adulthood." Columbus, Ohio: ERIC Clearinghouse on Adult, Career, and Vocational Education, Digest no. 200, 1998. (ED423426)

Lawrence, R. L. (ed.). *Artistic Ways of Knowing: Expanded Opportunities for Teaching and Learning.* New Directions for Adult and Continuing Education, no. 107. San Francisco: Jossey-Bass, 2005.

Mezirow, J. *Transformative Dimensions of Adult Learning.* San Francisco: Jossey-Bass, 1991.

Mezirow, J. "Learning to Think Like an Adult: Core Concepts of Transformation Theory." In J. Mezirow (ed.), *Learning as Transformation: Critical Perspectives on a Theory in Progress.* San Francisco: Jossey-Bass, 2000.

Schön, D. *The Reflective Practitioner: How Professionals Think in Action.* New York: Doubleday, 1983.

Tennant, M. C., and Pogson, P. *Learning and Change in the Adult Years: A Developmental Perspective.* San Francisco: Jossey-Bass, 1995.

Tisdell, E. J., Hanley, M. S., and Taylor, E. W. "Different Perspectives on Teaching for Critical Consciousness." In A. L. Wilson, E. R. Hayes (eds.), *Handbook of Adult and Continuing Education*. San Francisco: Jossey-Bass, 2000.

Yorks, L. "Adult Learning and the Generation of New Knowledge and Meaning: Creating Liberating Spaces for Fostering Adult Learning Through Practitioner-Based Collaborative Action Inquiry." *Teachers College Record*, 2005, *107*, 1217–1244.

Yorks, L., and Kasl, E. "Toward a Theory and Practice for Whole-Person Learning: Reconceptualizing Experience and the Role of Affect." *Adult Education Quarterly*, 2002, *52*, 176–192.

Yorks, L., and Kasl, E. "I Know More Than I Can Say: A Taxonomy for Utilizing Expressive Ways of Knowing to Foster Transformative Learning." *Journal of Transformative Education*, 2006, *4*(1), 1–22.

SANDRA HAYES is a lecturer in the Department of Organization and Leadership and a doctoral candidate in the Adult Learning and Leadership Program, Teachers College, Columbia University.

LYLE YORKS is an associate professor and director of the Adult Education Guided Intensive Study (AEGIS) doctoral program in the Department of Organization and Leadership, Teachers College, Columbia University.

INDEX

nonharassment and antidiscrimination policies; achieve domestic partner benefits; and build best practices into organizational strategies. It explores sexual identity development in the workplace through the lens of transformational learning theory and opens new ways to think about career development. In addition, this volume offers unique insights into lesbian issues in organizations, including the double bind of sexual orientation and gender discrimination. Some of the chapter authors look specifically at educational settings, such as the continuing professional development of K–12 teachers and the dynamics of dealing with sexual orientation in higher education, while others focus on business workplaces. The volume concludes with an analysis of public policies and organizational practices that are important to LGBTQ lives, with a focus on how organizational policy can make space for the emergence of difference related to sexual orientation and gender identity.
ISBN 0-7879-9495-2

ACE111 **Authenticity in Teaching**
Patricia Cranton
Authenticity is one of those concepts, like soul, spirit, or imagination, that is easier to define in terms of what it is not than what it is. We can fairly easily say that someone who lies to students or who pretends to know things he or she does not know or who deliberately dons a teaching persona is not authentic. But do the opposite behaviors guarantee authentic teaching? Not necessarily. Becoming an authentic teacher appears to be a developmental process that relies on experience, maturity, self-exploration, and reflection. It is the purpose of this volume to explore a variety of ways of thinking about authenticity in teaching, from the perspective of scholars who dedicate themselves to understanding adult education theory and research and from that of practitioners who see themselves as working toward authentic practice.

The contributors address five overlapping and interrelated dimensions of authenticity: self-awareness and self-exploration; awareness of others (especially students); relationships with students; awareness of cultural, social, and educational contexts and their influence on practice; and critical self-reflection on teaching.
ISBN 0-7879-9403-0

ACE110 **The Neuroscience of Adult Learning**
Sandra Johnson and Kathleen Taylor
Recent research developments have added much to our understanding of brain function. Though some neurobiologists have explored implications for learning, few have focused on learning in adulthood. This issue of New Directions for Adult and Continuing Education, *The Neuroscience of Adult Learning,* examines links between this emerging research and adult educators' practice. Now that it is possible to trace the pathways of the brain involved in various learning tasks, we can also explore which learning environments are likely to be most effective. Volume contributors include neurobiologists, educators, and clinical psychologists who have illuminated connections between how the brain functions and how to enhance learning. Among the topics explored here are basic brain architecture and "executive" functions of the brain, how learning can "repair" the effects of psychological trauma on the brain, effects of stress and emotions on learning, the centrality of experience to learning and construction of knowledge, the mentor-learner relationship, and

intersections between best practices in adult learning and current neurobiological discoveries. Although the immediate goal of this volume is to expand the discourse on teaching and learning practices, our overarching goal is to encourage adult learners toward more complex ways of knowing.
ISBN 0-7879-8704-2

ACE109 Teaching for Change: Fostering Transformative Learning in the Classroom
Edward W. Taylor
Fostering transformative learning is about teaching for change. It is not an approach to be taken lightly, arbitrarily, or without much thought. Many would argue that it requires intentional action, a willingness to take personal risk, a genuine concern for the learner's betterment, and the wherewithal to draw on a variety of methods and techniques that help create a classroom environment that encourages and supports personal growth. What makes the work of transformative learning even more difficult is the lack of clear signposts or guidelines that teachers can follow when they try to teach for change. There is now a need to return to the classroom and look through the lens of those who have been engaged in the practice of fostering transformative learning. This volume's authors are seasoned practitioners and scholars who have grappled with the fundamental issues associated with teaching for change (emotion, expressive ways of knowing, power, cultural difference, context, teacher authenticity, spirituality) in a formal classroom setting; introduced innovations that enhance the practice of fostering transformative learning; and asked ethical questions that need to be explored and reflected upon when practicing transformative learning in the classroom.
ISBN 0-7879-8584-8

ACE108 Adulthood: New Terrain
Mary Alice Wolf
One of the many surprises about the lifespan perspective is that individuals, families, institutions, and corporations lead *many* lives. The purpose of this resource is to acquaint and update practitioners in adult education and related roles with emerging and creative methods of 1) appreciating the learner's perspective, 2) moderating content and learning format to enhance meaning-making in the learning environment, and 3) developing tools to address alternative modes of development and growth that occur in adulthood and challenge adult educators on a daily basis.

What does the new adult learner look like? This volume contains theory and research on learners who turn to educational programs in times of transition and explores ways of connecting with new cognitive and affective meanings.

This volume explores dimensions of adult development from ethnographic, research, and theoretical perspectives. It addresses adult learners' experience and meaning of education as an ongoing resource for well-being and positive development across the lifecourse. It updates the reader in the emerging terrain of adulthood; adult learning philosophies are implemented and modified to meet adults' developmental mandate to continue learning in order to make meaning and find purpose during the countless transitions of the ever-increasing adult years.
ISBN 0-7879-8396-0

ACE107 Artistic Ways of Knowing: Expanded Opportunities for Teaching and Learning
Randee Lipson Lawrence
This volume of *New Directions for Adult and Continuing Education* challenges the dominant paradigm of how knowledge is typically constructed and shared in adult education settings by focusing on ways in which adult educators can expand learning opportunities and experiences for their learners. Art appeals universally to us all and has the capacity to bridge cultural differences. Art can also foster individual and social transformation, promoting dialogue and deepening awareness of ourselves and the world around us. The contributors to this volume include actors, musicians, photographers, storytellers, and poets, all of whom also happen to be adult educators. In each chapter, the author describes how one or more forms of artistic expression were used to promote learning in formal or informal adult education settings. In each case, the purpose of education was not to teach art (that is, not to develop expertise in acting, poetry writing, or creating great works of art). Conversely, art was used as a means to access learning in subjects as divergent as English language acquisition, action research, community awareness, and social justice.
ISBN 0-7879-8284-9

ACE106 Class Concerns: Adult Education and Social Class
Tom Nesbitt
This volume of *New Directions for Adult and Continuing Education* brings together several leading progressive adult educators to explore how class affects different arenas of adult education practice and discourse. It highlights the links between adult education, the material and social conditions of daily and working lives, and the economic and political systems that underpin them. Chapters focus on adult education policies; teaching; learning and identity formation; educational institutions and social movements; and the relationships between class, gender, and race. Overall, the volume reaffirms the salience of class in shaping the lives we lead and the educational approaches we develop. It offers suggestions for adult educators to identify and resist the encroachments of global capitalism and understand the role of education in promoting social equality. Finally, it suggests that a class perspective can provide an antidote to much of the social amnesia, self-absorption, and apolitical theorizing that pervades current adult education discourse.
ISBN 0-7879-8128-1

ACE105 HIV/AIDS Education for Adults
John P. Egan
Contributors from the United States, Canada, and Australia, working in university-based and community-based environments and for divergent communities, present specific experiences in the fight against HIV/AIDS. They share stories of shifting paradigms and challenging norms, and of seeking and finding innovation. Topics examined include the struggle for meaning and power in HIV/AIDS education, HIV prevention workers and injection drug users, community-based research, grassroots response to HIV/AIDS in Nova Scotia, sex workers and HIV/AIDS education, and the Tuskegee Syphilis Study and legacy recruitment for experimental vaccines. By examining HIV/AIDS through an adult education lens, we gain insights into how communities (and governments) can respond quickly and effectively to emergent health issues—and other issues linked to marginalization.
ISBN 0-7879-8032-3

New Directions for Adult & Continuing Education
Order Form
SUBSCRIPTIONS AND SINGLE ISSUES

DISCOUNTED BACK ISSUES:

Use this form to receive **20% off** all back issues of New Directions for Adult & Continuing Education. All single issues priced at **$23.20** (normally $29.00)

TITLE	ISSUE NO.	ISBN
_____	_____	_____
_____	_____	_____
_____	_____	_____

Call 888-378-2537 or see mailing instructions below. When calling, mention the promotional code, JB7ND, to receive your discount.

SUBSCRIPTIONS: *(1 year, 4 issues)*

☐ New Order   ☐ Renewal

U.S.	☐ Individual: $80	☐ Institutional: $195
Canada/Mexico	☐ Individual: $80	☐ Institutional: $235
All Others	☐ Individual: $104	☐ Institutional: $269

Call 888-378-2537 or see mailing and pricing instructions below. Online subscriptions are available at www.interscience.wiley.com.

Copy or detach page and send to:
John Wiley & Sons, Journals Dept, 5th Floor
989 Market Street, San Francisco, CA 94103-1741

Order Form can also be faxed to: 888-481-2665

Issue/Subscription Amount: $ _____	**SHIPPING CHARGES:**
Shipping Amount: $ _____	SURFACE Domestic Canadian
(for single issues only—subscription prices include shipping)	First Item $5.00 $6.00
Total Amount: $ _____	Each Add'l Item $3.00 $1.50

(No sales tax for U.S. subscriptions. Canadian residents, add GST for subscription orders. Individual rate subscriptions must be paid by personal check or credit card. Individual rate subscriptions may not be resold as library copies.)

☐ Payment enclosed (U.S. check or money order only. All payments must be in U.S. dollars.)

☐ VISA   ☐ MC   ☐ Amex # _____ Exp. Date_____

Card Holder Name _____ Card Issue # _____

Signature_____ Day Phone _____

☐ Bill Me (U.S. institutional orders only. Purchase order required.)

Purchase order # _____
Federal Tax ID13559302   GST 89102 8052

Name_____

Address _____

Phone _____ E-mail _____

JB7ND

Statement of Ownership, Management, and Circulation
(All Periodicals Publications Except Requester Publications)

1. Publication Title	2. Publication Number									3. Filing Date
New Directions for Adult and Continuing Education	1	0	5	2	_	2	8	9	1	10/1/2007

4. Issue Frequency	5. Number of Issues Published Annually	6. Annual Subscription Price
Quarterly	4	$209

7. Complete Mailing Address of Known Office of Publication (Not printer) (Street, city, county, state, and ZIP+4®)	Contact Person
Wiley Subscriptions Services, Inc. at Jossey-Bass, 989 Market St., San Francisco, CA 94103	Joe Schuman
	Telephone (Include area code) 415-782-3232

8. Complete Mailing Address of Headquarters or General Business Office of Publisher (Not printer)

Wiley Subscriptions Services, Inc., 111 River Street, Hoboken, NJ 07030

9. Full Names and Complete Mailing Addresses of Publisher, Editor, and Managing Editor (Do not leave blank)

Publisher (Name and complete mailing address)

Wiley Subscriptions Services, Inc., A Wiley Company at San Francisco, 989 Market St., San Francisco, CA 94103-1741

Editor (Name and complete mailing address)

Susan Imel, Ohio State University/Eric-Acve, 1900 Kenny Road, Columbus, OH 43210-1090

Managing Editor (Name and complete mailing address)

Co-editor - Jovita M. Ross-Gordon, Texas State University, EAPS Department, San Marcos, TX 78666

10. Owner (Do not leave blank. If the publication is owned by a corporation, give the name and address of the corporation immediately followed by the names and addresses of all stockholders owning or holding 1 percent or more of the total amount of stock. If not owned by a corporation, give the names and addresses of the individual owners. If owned by a partnership or other unincorporated firm, give its name and address as well as those of each individual owner. If the publication is published by a nonprofit organization, give its name and address.)

Full Name	Complete Mailing Address
Wiley Subscriptions Services	111 River Street, Hoboken, NJ
(see attached list)	

11. Known Bondholders, Mortgagees, and Other Security Holders Owning or Holding 1 Percent or More of Total Amount of Bonds, Mortgages, or Other Securities. If none, check box ▸ ☑ None

Full Name	Complete Mailing Address

12. Tax Status (For completion by nonprofit organizations authorized to mail at nonprofit rates) (Check one)
The purpose, function, and nonprofit status of this organization and the exempt status for federal income tax purposes:
☐ Has Not Changed During Preceding 12 Months
☐ Has Changed During Preceding 12 Months (Publisher must submit explanation of change with this statement)

PS Form **3526**, September 2006 (Page 1 of 3 (Instructions Page 3)) PSN 7530-01-000-9931 PRIVACY NOTICE: See our privacy policy on www.usps.com

13. Publication Title	14. Issue Date for Circulation Data
New Directions for Adult and Continuing Education	Summer 2007

15. Extent and Nature of Circulation			Average No. Copies Each Issue During Preceding 12 Months	No. Copies of Single Issue Published Nearest to Filing Date
a. Total Number of Copies (Net press run)			1274	1208
b. Paid Circulation (By Mail and Outside the Mail)	(1)	Mailed Outside-County Paid Subscriptions Stated on PS Form 3541(include paid copies, and exchange copies)	451	430
	(2)	Mailed In-County Paid Subscriptions Stated on PS Form 3541 (Include paid distribution above nominal rate, advertiser's proof copies, and exchange copies)	0	0
	(3)	Paid Distribution Outside the Mails Including Sales Through Dealers and Carriers, Street Vendors, Counter Sales, and Other Paid Distribution Outside USPS®	0	0
	(4)	Paid Distribution by Other Classes of Mail Through the USPS (e.g. First-Class Mail®)	0	0
c. Total Paid Distribution (Sum of 15b (1), (2),(3), and (4))			451	430
d. Free or Nominal Rate Distribution (By Mail and Outside the Mail)	(1)	Free or Nominal Rate Outside-County Copies Iincluded on PS Form 3541	0	0
	(2)	Free or Nominal Rate In-County Copies Included on PS Form 3541	0	0
	(3)	Free or Nominal Rate Copies Mailed at Other Classes Through the USPS (e.g. First-Class Mail)	0	0
	(4)	Free or Nominal Rate Distribution Outside the Mail (Carriers or other means)	68	67
e. Total Free or Nominal Rate Distribution (Sum of 15d (1), (2), (3) and (4))			68	67
f. Total Distribution (Sum of 15c and 15e)			519	497
g. Copies not Distributed (See Instructions to Publishers #4 (page #3))			755	711
h. Total (Sum of 15f and g)			1274	1208
i. Percent Paid (15c divided by 15f times 100)			87%	87%

16. Publication of Statement of Ownership

☑ If the publication is a general publication, publication of this statement is required. Will be printed in the WINTER 2007 issue of this publication.   ☐ Publication not required.

17. Signature and Title of Editor, Publisher, Business Manager, or Owner	Date
Susan E. Lewis, VP & Publisher - Periodicals [signature]	10/1/2007

I certify that all information furnished on this form is true and complete. I understand that anyone who furnishes false or misleading information on this form or who omits material or information requested on the form may be subject to criminal sanctions (including fines and imprisonment) and/or civil sanctions (including civil penalties).

PS Form **3526**, September 2006 (Page 2 of 3)